WHY DO PEOPLE HATE AMERICA?

Ziauddin Sardar
Merryl Wyn Davies

MJF BOOKS
NEW YORK

Published by MJF Books
Fine Communications
322 Eighth Avenue
New York, NY 10001

Why Do People Hate America?
LC Control Number 2004117592
ISBN 1-56731-721-9

Copyright © 2002 Ziauddin Sardar & Merryl Wyn Davies
Foreword Copyright © 2003

This special edition is published by MJF Books by arrangement with The
Disinformation Company Ltd. First published in Great Britain by Icon Books Ltd.

All rights reserved. No part of this publication may be reproduced or transmit-
ted in any form or by any means, electronic or mechanical, including photocopy,
recording, or any information storage and retrieval system, without the prior
written permission of the publisher.

Manufactured in the United States of America on acid-free paper ∞

MJF Books and the MJF colophon are trademarks of Fine Creative Media, Inc.

QM   10   9   8   7   6   5   4   3   2   1

Contents

Foreword

The question "Why do people hate America?" has become even more pertinent after the war in Iraq. Indeed, since our book was first published on July 4, 2002, it has acquired a universal dimension. The question has been addressed by global opinion polls; and commentators and newspaper columnists across the five continents have wondered how, in less than two years after the atrocity of 9-11, a moment of universal sympathy for America has been transformed into a growing fissure not only in public attitudes but in basic institutions of the world order. As a statement, "Why people hate America" has been taken up as a rallying cry by politicians and commentators of right and left and turned into a call to the barricades. It has served to justify a mutually sustaining cycle of reaction. As a widely accepted fact, hatred of America has been wielded to generate support for, or unexamined acceptance of, actions and initiatives that have entrenched the problem of America, made it more intractable, less open to reasoned debate, and made the USA more intent on pursuing its own course irrespective of the increasing disquiet, fear and antipathy caused. As one review noted, subsequent events "virtually parod[y] the argument" we made (Future Survey 25 (3), March 12, 2003).

In short, before, during and after the war on Iraq, America has acted and reacted in accordance with the premises we analysed as the causes for concern. And the consequences can be read in the headline results of global surveys of opinion. The Washington-based Pew Research Centre for People and the Press survey published in June 2003 found: "opinions of the US are markedly lower than they were last year. The war has widened the rift between Americans and Western Europeans, further inflamed the Muslim world, softened support for the war on terrorism, and significantly weakened global public support for the pillars of the post-World War II era—the UN and the North Atlantic alliance" (mailprc@people-press.org).

A survey of eleven countries conducted by the BBC in conjunction with various polling organizations found 60% of respondents outside the US had unfavourable or fairly unfavourable attitudes towards the American President. Respondents in all countries except Australia, Israel and the United States rated America as more dangerous than Syria, a potential next candidate to join the "Axis of Evil." The poll also showed negative attitudes to the war on terrorism and US efforts in the Middle East.

Beyond the headlines are more disturbing results. The earlier Pew Global Attitudes survey, published in March 2003, found less than 40% of respondents in Western Europe endorse the spread of American ideas and customs, and less than 50% like American ideas about democracy. A European Union survey of attitudes published early in 2003 found widespread support in European countries for the proposition that America is responsible for harming the environment and operates to keep poor countries poor. More tellingly, Pew surveys found that in the years leading up to September 11, 2001 only 30% of Americans claimed to be very interested in news about other countries. The trauma of 9-11 has produced no change. In September 2002, only about 26% of Americans surveyed said they followed foreign news "very closely," while 45% said international events did not affect them.

In its response to 9-11, America has shown itself to be not only a hyperpower but increasingly assertive and ready to use its dominance as a hyperpower. After declaring a War on Terrorism, America has led two conventional wars, in Afghanistan and Iraq, demonstrating its overwhelmingly awesome military might. But these campaigns reveal something more: America's willingness to have recourse to arms as appropriate and legitimate means to secure its interests and bolster its security. It has set forth a new doctrine: the right of pre-emptive strike when it considers its security, and therefore its national interests, to be at risk. The essence of this doctrine is the real meaning of hyperpower.

Prime Minister Tony Blair has consistently argued that the only option in the face of hyperpower is to offer wise counsel. But increasingly this is a course that governments and people across the world have refused. The mobilisation for war against Iraq split the United Nations and provoked the largest anti-war demonstrations the world has ever seen. And through it all, America maintained its determination to wage war alone if necessary and not to be counselled by the concerns of supposedly allied governments when they faithfully represented the wishes of their electorates.

Rather than engaging in debate, the American government expressed its exasperation. The influential new breed of neo-conservative radio and television hosts went much further. They acted as ringmasters for outpourings of public scorn that saw French fries renamed "freedom fries" and moves to boycott French and German produce across America. If one sound-bite can capture a mood, then perhaps it would be from Fox News' Bill O'Reilly. At the height of the tension over a second Security Council resolution to legitimate war in Iraq, Mr O'Reilly told his viewers that the bottom line was security, the security of his family, and in that matter "There's no moral equivalence between the US and Belgium." It is, in effect, the ethos of hyperpower articulated and made manifest in the public domain of 24-hour talk.

And America's willingness to prosecute war has raised innumerable questions about how it engages with other countries. Afghanistan has seen the removal of the Taliban. But there are no official statistics on the number of innocent civilians dead and injured to achieve that security objective. The people of Afghanistan have witnessed a descent into the chaos that preceded the arrival of the Taliban, a country administered not by a new era of democracy under the tutelage of the hyperpower, but merely by the return of the warlords. Beyond Kabul, much of the country remains too insecure for any meaningful efforts at reconstruction and there is enormous difficulty in bringing relief aid to the rural population.

In Iraq, major conflict was swiftly declared ended. But, at the time of going to press, Iraqis know neither peace nor security as the vacuum of power continues to generate chaos. America's plans for nation-building have shown themselves to be self-serving of American economic and strategic interests rather than the self-determined wishes of the Iraqi people. America has made abundantly clear its determination to secure the privatisation of swathes of the Iraqi economy, with contracts awarded without open tender to major US corporations—many with close links to the Bush White House—that will foreclose the options for whatever government eventually emerges in Iraq.

Beyond the matters of war and national security, substantive issues across the whole spectrum that we explored have continued to accumulate. Whether it is protection for American steelmakers, refusal to acknowledge the scientific consensus on global warming, refusal to participate in the establishment of an International Criminal Court, abrogating the ABM treaty to move ahead with the Star Wars initiative, or using government power to promote and defend the interests of manufacturers of genetically modified crops against the distaste and disquiet of consumers in Europe and even the hungry in poor nations of the Third World, America has continued to exert its power for narrow national self interest.

Our purpose in this book was not to rehearse the grounds for complaint against America, but to analyse how the important issues that divide people and provide reasons for why people hate America emerge as a coherent expression of the American self-image. Mere complaint can never lead to a constructive debate. Debate and dialogue with America is never simply a matter of straightforward politics, or a discussion of moral imperatives. The dialogue has a context that involves the national myth and the historic narratives that form the self-image of the United States. Issues of war, trade, and foreign policy are understood in a cultural context, encoded and decoded in light of history and the "home truths" of American national myths.

The connections were as evident in American rhetoric and reaction in the run-up to war in Iraq as in the declaration of the end of hostilities. Invective against France is a case in point. In news broadcasts and talk shows, American veterans of World War II repeatedly expressed their disgust at French opposition to American plans in the Security Council. To understand the significance that these old soldiers placed on the battlefields of Europe, one needs to read our analysis of the film *Shane*. The spilling of American blood in France is read against, and in many respects is seen as an extension o, that cinematic classic of homesteading. In America, the spilling of blood signifies and legitimates possession of the land. The hero employs violence to make the land safe for the simple virtues of democracy on behalf of, and for the benefit of, simple homesteaders unable to protect themselves from lawless tyrants. In World War II and in American re-telling of that history, America brought the ethic of its western narrative to the conflict in Europe.

The possession that this sacrifice legitimated was loyalty, allegiance, a kind of fealty to American virtue, the real source of its supremacy, the rationale for America as hyperpower. In a deep and real sense, Americans expected not debate and reasoned argument from France, but unswerving support for American policy. The potency of this national outlook is the source of the mutual incomprehension between Americans and the French. For Americans, politicians and public alike, it was not simply a matter of difference over strategic policy. The issue was simultaneously a fundamental difference over values, creed and the duties and obligations arising from them.

The carefully prepared scene for the declaration of the end of hostilities in Iraq made this link with national ethos as expounded in popular culture both clear and facilely banal. President George W. Bush invoked the imagery of Hollywood to emphasise what victory—"we have prevailed"—should mean to America. In homage to a scene from the blockbuster movie *Independence Day*, President Bush helped to pilot the plane that landed on the aircraft carrier Abraham Lincoln. He climbed from the plane clad in the flight gear of a combat pilot to embrace similarly clad aircrew on the deck of the carrier. The imagery was instantly recognisable, and commented upon in the media both in America and abroad.

In the movie *Independence Day*, a youthful President, a former air force officer, returns to combat status and takes to the air to lead his troops in defeating an alien enemy that is utterly, incomprehensibly, irredeemably evil. In amazing special effects sequences, the enemy is shown maliciously destroying the skyscrapers of New York and blowing up the White House. It is not necessary to have seen the movie *Independence Day* to appreciate the parallels the White House press office was subtly invoking. It is necessary to remember that the movie concerns a global conflict and hence a global victory, and concludes with the line that, in the future, July 4th is Independence Day for the whole world.

We analyze these films not for the purpose of artistic criticism, but to examine what these products of American popular culture tell us about America's self-image and its understanding of the world, to analyse the links between image and ideas and to question how they influence attitudes to the crucial issues of America's real military, political, economic and cultural relations with the rest of the world. The political discourse of America has been alive with references and recourse to national myth and historic narrative in the years since 9-11. A Texan President has frequently employed the language of the western to express his policy and ideas.

In a recent article in *Foreign Policy* ("The Paradoxes of American Nationalism"), Minxin Pei of the Carnegie Endowment for International Peace argued that America is characterised by a strong and paradoxical nationalism. "American nationalism is hidden in plain sight. But even if Americans saw it, they wouldn't recognise it as nationalism", Pei argues. American nationalism is clothed in the creed of democratic values and virtues, expressed in myth and historic narrative, expounded in the products of American popular culture, exported around the world and seen as the future inheritance of all peoples. To create the ground for debate and engagement with America, the particularity of its nationalism, the national self-absorption in its myth and historic narrative, have to be subjected to analysis. Without analysis there is only the continuing mutual incomprehension of the World War II veterans and the mass of the French public.

American popular culture creates stereotypes and exports them around the world. But, as we also argue, America is not an open market for the cultural products of other countries. It is easy to build a stereotype of America as an insular, self-absorbed nation of continental proportions that knows little or nothing about the rest of the world. One overriding American response to criticism and dissent over the war in Iraq was to say: "So what? I just don't care what the rest of the world thinks." Yet, as we try to make clear throughout this book, America cannot be reduced to such a simplistic stereotype. It contains debate, difference of opinion and criticism of its role and activities abroad. The peace movement was as active in America as across Europe and beyond in the run-up to war in Iraq. There is no lack of American critics of America, its policy, actions and its sustaining myths. The problem is how marginalised and submerged they have been in the mainstream of American discourse, another reality hidden in plain sight. Perhaps one of the most troubling effects of the trauma of 9-11 on America has been the narrowing of the already reduced ambit of national debate, accompanied by the acknowledged self-censorship of the American media.

Veteran CBS news anchor Dan Rather has acknowledged as much, but did so only when interviewed in Britain. At times during the war in Iraq, it seemed as if American and British audiences were watching and hearing about a different war. They have certainly been watching a different "peace." Britons with access to satellite programmes can regularly watch America's three television network news broadcasts as well as the two 24-hour cable news networks. Americans have no comparable access to how the world or America is seen by other nations. The questions routinely asked by the British media about the war and the progress of the "peace" are largely absent from American television news broadcasts. An open society with the most powerful broadcast media in the world is starved of critical, investigative reporting. Creating new constituencies of debate across nations is not only a matter of overcoming what we define as "knowledgeable ignorance," but is also a matter of information deficit.

Our purpose in this book is to argue that hatred is the worst possible basis for human relations, especially relations between nations. It is our contention that hatred dehumanises everyone and makes all problems more intractable. Hatred is never simply one-way traffic. It is a relational, reactive condition. It affects how judgments are made about what actions are permissible, appropriate and warranted on both sides of a mutual divide of distrust. It can become a mutually sustained cycle of defensive reaction, a self-fulfilling and self-perpetuating prophecy.

So, we need to go beyond hatred. The problem of America is everyone's problem. Finding an answer depends on making visible the nature, conditions and dimensions of the problem so that new debates, new constituencies of dissent that bridge the divide between America and the rest of the world, can be built. As the war on Iraq showed, the questions we raise and issues we analyse in this book have become more urgent and pertinent. It is our hope that future events will utilise the analysis and arguments we present to find viable solutions and remedies and lay the foundations for a truly peaceful world.

Introduction

As the dust cloud settled over Lower Manhattan on 11 Sept-ember 2001, an unnamed, shell-shocked woman emerged from the swirling gloom around the Twin Towers. Her words to a waiting television reporter were not 'Why?', a simple expression of incomprehension, but a focused and pained question: 'Why do they hate us?' Her words were instantly taken up by everyone. They were addressed by President Bush, by politicians and commentators, they appeared in newspapers and magazines, were heard again and again on television and radio, and have been on the lips of people on the street and in their homes across America. And the same question has been asked far beyond the USA.

With constant repetition, these words have been subtly transformed. The question has acquired the status of fact, a statement whose meaning can be assumed, rather than a basis for inquiry. The need to know has been transformed into a reason not to know.

In April 2002, Britain's veteran Middle East correspondent, Robert Fisk, made a lecture tour of America. An outspoken critic of US Middle East policy, he chose a talk with the deliberately provocative title: 'September 11: ask who did it, but for heaven's sake don't ask why.' And for the first time in a decade of giving such lectures, he was shocked to encounter packed audiences who expressed an 'extraordinary new American refusal to go along with the official line, the growing, angry awareness among Americans that they were being lied to and deceived'.[1] Never before, he reports, had he been asked by

Americans, 'How can we make our press report the Middle East fairly?', or – much more disturbingly – 'How can we make our government reflect *our* views?' And then there was the retired US naval officer who recounted his personal experience from the 1973 Middle East war before reflecting on Israel's 2002 invasion of Palestinian Authority territory: 'When I see on television our planes and our tanks used to attack Palestinians, I can understand why people hate Americans.'[2]

We focus on the question – 'Why do people hate America?' – as a question, not as a statement. We examine its terms of reference and take it as an honest, earnest and impassioned demand that recognises a communication gap, an information deficit.

This is not a book about 9-11; nor is it about the action stemming from it. It is a book prompted by that awful event and concerned to understand the overriding question that emerged from the devastation. It is not about 9-11 because the question that those horrific events produced requires an examination of problems that existed before that criminal act, problems that would have continued to exist irrespective of such a crime. True, they are now compounded and made more urgent and volatile, but this is partly because the events of 9-11 have not prompted diligent inquiry and serious debate, but a resort to the very agenda that constructs the problem of relations between America and the rest of the world in the first place. We turn our attention to the background and context, not to evade discussing the response, but because unless the background is revealed and made part of the debate, there is little hope of making more informed decisions.

This is also not a book about the positive sides of the United States: those looking for a straightforward counterblast to the hatred expressed for America should stop reading now. It is a book about the consequences of interaction in a world in which gross disparities of power, wealth, freedom and opportunity must be factored into each and every situation. In such an interconnected globe, both good and bad intentions shape the domestic character of a nation and its consequent relationship with the rest of the world. One of the main points we make in this book is that many of the worst effects of American power are the result of the best-intentioned actions. As a result, the animosity in other parts of the world often seems unaccountable to the US, and this makes it difficult for well-meaning Americans to conceive of an effective change in policy. We focus on the effects of US policy, past and present, on the wider world; and we draw examples, in particular, from the developing world. These effects are matters of concern not only to people of the Third World, but also to many in Europe as well as in the US itself, such as the anti-globalisation protestors and numerous movements for justice and peace. However, we argue that a more careful and imaginative approach to US foreign policy is essential if worldwide anti-American feeling is not to spiral out of control. By setting out clearly what makes people hate America, we hope to show what those new policies need to address.

If the question of why people hate America is not new, it has acquired a new resonance since the events of 9-11. In particular, it brought out the sharp division between the politics of left and right – a distinction that had all but collapsed in the 1990s under the influence of 'liberalisation' and 'globalisation'. And it dredged up the age-old and deep-seated prejudices that exist about Muslims and Islam in Western society in general and in the United States in particular.

In the discussion of 9-11 in the American media, the basic premises of the question were taken for granted. As the *Boston Globe*'s Beverly Beckham declared, one thing is clear: 'They hate us, these people from a culture we don't know and don't understand and never gave much thought to until now.' Moreover, she contended, this hatred is not like any other. 'We have people who hate right in our own back yard, whole groups of haters, who lash out against blacks and gays and Catholics and Jews. But this hate directed at ALL Americans is bigger and deadlier because it's fuelled by rage that is calculated, then unleashed, no matter what the cost.'[3] As we shall see in chapter one, Beckham echoed the general consensus of much media coverage on both sides of the Atlantic.

So, 'Why do people hate America?' is a loaded question. It assumes that there is a monolithic 'America' that is the object of an equally monumental hatred. It assumes that this hatred flows in one direction only: 'people' out there 'hate America' and 'all Americans', but America itself is a benevolent entity. In chapter two, we ask whether there is something in the nature of the question itself that produces polarisation. By analysing and placing the question in a broader, historical context, we hope to determine what makes a meaningful answer.

As Robert Fisk makes clear, there is more diversity of opinion within America than the official image of rallying round the flag would suggest. We are acutely aware that America is not a monolith, a fact that we try to reflect throughout this book, even as we explore and question the self-image of America founded on the proposition of its national motto: 'E pluribus unum' ('from many, one'). Equally, we are conscious that we use the word 'America', as everyone else does, repeatedly and indiscriminately. Like the 19th-century 'Monroe Doctrine', this unconscious usage ascribes all of the Americas as the natural sphere of interest of just one of its nation states, the USA. That everyone understands the word 'America' to refer to the USA is a testimony to power founded on a wealth of resources, economic strength and its application to an idea of nationhood that is unique. It is the nature of that uniqueness, and how it impacts on the wider world, that is the subject of this book.

The indiscriminate use of the term 'America' to cover many and different aspects of US influence and operation around the world is a reflection of what we define as the 'hamburger syndrome'. By this we mean that while the rest of the world experiences America through many different channels – political and foreign policy, military action, the work of the intelligence services, cultural products, the media, consumer and lifestyle products, business corporations, aid agencies and non-governmental organisations, educational institutions – there is a coherence and interrelationship between them all. A hamburger comes as a package: it is a meal in itself; it is produced, sold and eaten in a particular way; the entire system is an integral part of the hamburger experience. It is not possible to take one part and leave aside another. You may decide to take the pickle, tomato or lettuce out of the hamburger, but you bought them all together, you paid for them, were given all of them and have to do something about them, whether you want them or not.

America – in its actions and effect on other people around the world – forms an immensely coherent whole. Wherever Americans travel, they take that complex whole with them and operate within its terms of reference. If the rest of the world fails to make distinctions between the various aspects of America, then it is doing no more than America itself has insisted must be done. In chapters three and four, we confront this question directly. Through an examination of American foreign and economic policies, its treatment of the rest of the world at the United Nations, its control of global institutions such as the International Monetary Fund and World Trade Organisation, and its relationship with developing countries over the last five decades, we explore the rationale for the grievances of the rest of the world against America. Moreover, we examine the way in which the brand called 'America' has been sold to the rest of the world, and the consequences of the globalisation of American culture on the developing countries.

Most Americans are simply not aware of the impact of their culture and their government's policies on the rest of the world. But, more important, a vast majority simply do not believe that America has done, or can do, anything wrong. A poll of world 'opinion leaders' in politics, media, business, culture and government, commissioned by the Paris-based *International Herald Tribune*, revealed that a majority of non-US respondents – 58%

– felt that Washington's policies were a 'major cause' in fuelling resentment and anger against the United States. In contrast, only 18% of US respondents blamed their government's policies. Moreover, 90% of Americans listed their country's power and wealth as the chief reason why they are disliked, while the non-Americans overwhelmingly thought that the US bears responsibility for the gap between the world's rich and poor. The poll suggested that 'much of the world views the attacks as a symptom of increasingly bitter polarization between haves and have-nots'; and that America is largely responsible for developing countries 'missing out on the spoils of economic progress'.[4]

Why are the perceptions of Americans so far apart from those of the rest of the world? Why are presumptions of innocence and self-righteousness so central to the American self-image? In chapters five and six, we locate America's image of itself in its historic narratives and founding myths; and in the idea of the American Hero, who has, as John Wayne is always mimicked as saying, 'got to do what a man's got to do'. We argue that definitions are relational terms, that our image of ourselves includes, and in part depends on, our view of other people. It is the relational nature of America that especially concerns us. The idea of America, its self-image and sense of identity, uniquely, has always been less concerned with history than with a vision of the future that requires a particular way of operating in the present. In particular, we are concerned that America's idealised view of the human future permits a perverse, dangerous and often brutally destructive disconnection between ends and means. To define the idea of America as *the* future, everyone's future, is an arrogant denial of the freedom of others, and of the potential of the present to create alternative futures in the complex image of the whole world and all its peoples.

No society is more open than America, more blessed with the means of communication, the resources to learn and to know, to express and project its ideas. Yet the product of this enormous American infrastructure – its media – is intensely inward looking and self-absorbed. The rest of the world also learns about and experiences America through its media, especially Hollywood, whose works are shaped by American consciousness and outlook. Films and television have now become the main tools of representation as well as the media through which the world thinks – or, more frequently, does not think – and perceives. We thus make no apology for enveloping much of our analysis in films and television programmes, since a deeper understanding of our central question requires us to go beyond conventional politics and look also at the cultural and representational straitjackets encasing the globe. And the power of the American media, as we repeatedly argue, works to keep American people closed to experience and ideas from the rest of the world and thereby increases the insularity, self-absorption and ignorance that is the overriding problem the rest of the world has with America.

America is what we have termed a 'hyperpower' – a nation so powerful that it affects the lives of people everywhere. Yet, Americans are shielded from knowledge and debate about the actual consequences of US engagement with the rest of the world. Time and again in the televised town meetings in the first days after 9-11, ordinary Americans themselves acknowledged this fact. Power without informed democratic control and oversight is not responsible. It is not an expression of 'Right', and can become a recipe for conniving in wrongs done in one's name, without one's consent, and against what would, on calm reflection, be one's better judgement.

The events of 9-11 were a major trauma for the American psyche. They have spawned innumerable courses and classroom initiatives at all levels of the US education system. It is one of our central arguments that at the heart of relations between America and the rest of the world stands a problem of knowledge. In precise terms, we call it the problem of 'knowledgeable ignorance': knowing people, ideas, civilisations, religions, histories as something they are not, and could not possibly be, and maintaining these ideas even when the means exist to know differently. Knowledgeable ignorance is a term applied to the Western view of Islam and Muslims in particular. It refers to more than general negative attitudes and ideas; it defines the way in which such attitudes are built into an approach to knowledge, a body of study and expertise called Orientalism.

This problem of knowledge is not exclusive to America; it is a general feature of Western civilisation, and it has a considerable history. What the West turns to and takes for knowledge of the non-West – learned opinion and scholarly evidence – is itself the problem. For the USA, its own ideas and history are the only yardstick for what is reasonable, normal or proper, which means that America *constructs* what it knows about other cultures in binary opposition of 'like' and 'not like'. By this means, America comes to think that it knows best what is the nature, character and meaning of other peoples. But what has been amassed is a partial judgement based on self-interested, self-serving analysis that can produce only double standards.

In the response to 9-11, double standards founded on knowledgeable ignorance have been much in evidence. We argue that this problem of knowledge must be addressed, and that it can be overturned only by listening to, and deferring to, what other people have to say about themselves. Within the cultures of the developing countries, and their diaspora within the West, there is diversity, different shades of opinion, multiple schools of thought and numerous debates. Neither Islam nor any other non-Western civilisation is a monolith. More importantly, these civilisations are neither inflexible nor defined solely by ancient history. They are all living traditions seeking constantly to adapt, accommodate change, react and develop within their own terms, according to their own experience, values and ideas. While knowledgeable ignorance acts as the gatekeeper of what it is relevant and necessary to know about Third World civilisations, rather than listening to what they have to say of themselves, mutual understanding can never emerge.

America has constructed a vision of an 'axis of evil', a hostile, inimical perversion, endemic and hiding not just within a few nations but in communities spread across much of the world. Terror, terrorism and terrorists have become one single, simple, indistinguishable scourge of all humanity, shorn of political, social, historical or cultural roots and distinctions. This form of grand absolutism has its reflection; it is mirrored by a vision of America as a hostile, inimical perversion, endemic and operating within other nations all around the globe. This is a recipe for disaster. It is the basis for dehumanising and demonising relations in a world that is growing ever more interconnected. The only security and hope can come from learning and knowing ourselves and the rest of the world afresh, by placing what other people know of themselves in equal prominence.

America has the power and resources to refuse self-reflection. More pointedly, it is a nation that has developed a tradition of being oblivious to self-reflection. Yet, America is also a nation that produces strident self-criticism and many strands of dissenting opinion from writers, artists, academics, professionals and even politicians. Throughout the book we make it our practice to quote from among them. The problem for the rest of the world – and as Robert Fisk reports, increasingly for many Americans – is how little of the diversity of American opinion is reflected in the political discourse of governance, in Congress, and in the media. Within the US it often seems that the hardest topic to debate is the idea of America itself and its problems, let alone whether that idea may need to be adapted or improved in any way. However much frustration this creates in the US, it is the prime reason for infuriation, antipathy, hostility and even hatred beyond the bounds of America. If America cannot reflect upon itself, its history, its uses and abuses of power and wealth at home and abroad, the consequences of its lifestyle and abundance, the relations between quality of life and values, the relation between ideals and practical application of those ideals to all of its people, then what chance has the rest of the world of engaging America in reasoned discussion?

Hatred, of course, is no basis for building a secure world. In chapter seven we provide a thematic summary of why Americans have become, to quote a post-11 September banner in Pakistan, 'the most hated people on Earth'. And we explore ways by which we – all of us, Americans and non-Americans alike – can transcend hatred and work towards more viable and desirable futures.

We have crossed the threshold of the 21st century to greater mutual danger, with a more awful toll of human pain and suffering, than seemed possible. In all the violence and abhorrence that dominates the world, only one thing seems clear. We all have – as individuals and communities, Americans and non-Americans – a responsibility for the predicament and dangers facing the world. We all have a duty to think, act and work together; there is work to be done within each society to resolve hatred and build the possibility of peaceful cohabitation. We hope that this book is a small step in that hopeful direction.

CHAPTER ONE

Standing at Ground Zero

The picture of a plane swooping through a clear blue sky, tilting as it makes its approach to the elegant symmetry of a glass tower and then exploding in vibrant flame, has become a defining image of the 21st century. We witnessed that moment, and all the devastation that followed, live on television. The whole world experienced the catastrophe of 9-11 through the power and global reach of TV. Today, what we know of the world around us is mediated by television – now the first port of call for news, information and entertainment everywhere. We live in a world of images, packaged visual stories that come to us, and at us, wherever we turn – on billboards, in newspapers and magazines, on television, in the cinema – and we read into the images more than the pictures tell. This one defining image is horrific and real. It is not lessened just because it is effortlessly associated in our visual memory with the many unreal, fictional images of disaster that we have seen in films and on television. The important question is how much our response to the image of reality – our efforts to come to terms with the meaning of a real event – is shaped and structured by those associations. What are the links between the real and unreal images that shape our relations with the world in which we live?

Our direct personal experience of the world remains circumscribed: the neighbourhood in which we live, the place where we work, the schools that our children attend, the places where we shop, or worship, or go for entertainment, and the way we travel between them. This is the world of our daily round, as it was for all the generations that came before us. What makes our world smaller, more interconnected, is less the kind of lives we lead than the reach of communications technology that brings us vicarious experience – knowledge and ideas about what is beyond our individual experience – and brings it right into our homes. Television and the cultural products that it carries have become as significant a part of our lives as those things that we experience by direct personal contact. Our sense of identity, of belonging to larger communities, our cultural experiences, beliefs and opinions are shaped not only by the direct contacts of our daily lives but also by the larger world that we experience through the media. That the world saw and experienced 9-11 through television is only one small part of the story. How people everywhere have come to terms with that event, responded to it and been affected by it, is also mediated by the cultural community, the cultural conventions and communal resource of the media. Television showed us what happened; it also shows us the ways in which we thought about what happened.

The television series *The West Wing* represents the best of American liberal values and democratic culture. It won nine Emmies in its first season (more than any other programme, ever) and has been described by *Time* magazine as 'a national civics lesson'.[1] The continuing story of President Bartlet, a liberal Democrat of impeccable credentials, the show presents a parallel universe of US politics and a virtual mirror of American liberal consciousness. Just like any real administration in the White House, President Bartlet and his staff struggle to cope with personal problems, scandals, lobby groups, ethical dilemmas of power, domestic issues and global politics. On 3 October 2001, barely three weeks after the terrorist attacks on New York and Washington, NBC aired a special edition of *The West Wing*. The episode is a dramatised depiction, a creative – in the sense of imaginary – attempt to come to terms with real events. *The West*

Wing does not bring the real 9-11 into its virtual world – that would be an effrontery too far. But it does not need to; we all know what this episode is about. What is important is the way in which the programme deals with the issues.

The episode switches between two storylines. A group of high school students, part of a programme called Presidential Classroom, are caught up in a security alert while visiting the White House. They are directed to the Mess – 'its where we eat lunch' – a location provided with tables and chairs and a white board, where the series' cast of characters provides the lesson for the day. The second storyline is about an Arab American member of the White House staff, named Raqim Ali, who is suspected of terrorist links and bundled into a darkened room for urgent questioning. When Leo McGarry, the Chief of Staff, is informed that a potential terrorist may be on the premises, he looks stunned and mutters: 'Well ... it was only a matter of time, huh?' The menace of terrorism is more than a potential threat – it is an inevitable event merely waiting to happen, intent on reaching into the centre of American life, virtual or real. Counterpoised with the civics lesson, this alternate plot theme will be an evocation of actual response, a disturbing and robust encounter of raw emotion.

The civics lesson begins with a slightly oblique question to the one on everyone's mind. One of the students asks Josh Lyman, Deputy Chief of Staff: 'So ... what's the deal with everyone trying to kill you?' In the parallel universe of *The West Wing*, a previous storyline had Lyman critically injured when gunmen opened fire on the Presidential party during a visit to Virginia. Presidents are always in the line of fire, and *The West Wing* acknowledged the fact with a two-part story that opened its second season: 'In the Shadow of the Gunman', first aired on 4 October 2000. In that instance, the intended target was not the President but his daughter Zoë. The reason for the assassination: Zoë is dating Charlie Young, an aide to President Bartlet, who happens to be black. The gunmen are members of a neo-Nazi group called

West Virginia White Pride. It seems rather strange to refer to a previous episode within the fictional timeline when what we are about to receive is a special offering designed to stand explicitly outside that timeline. In the conventions of series television, such references set a context: in this case, the context of terror. It makes three connections. First, obviously, it makes the point that terror can have an American incarnation, that hatred is not an exclusive preserve of only one kind of group or society. On another level, it appears to be implying that racial hatred is the most pernicious and enduring of hatreds, an idea that we shall find at the heart of the special episode. Secondly, it provides an opportunity, through a long digression on the part of Lyman, to acknowledge the human impact of violence. In a world in which people feel as strongly, if not more so, about fictional characters than real ones, it is a means of incorporating emotion, however trite that may seem in the circumstances. Thirdly, possibly, we are getting a slight nod to the prescience of the series or the underlining of a simple fact: terror always has its own most obvious usual suspects. In the earlier episode, as the White House Situation Room is scrambling to deal with the shooting, the status report begins by noting that the whereabouts of Osama bin Laden are not immediately known, and there is concern about a front-line build-up of Iraqi Revolutionary Guards.

Once these references have been made, the special episode moves swiftly to the obvious question: 'So why is everyone trying to kill us?' As convenor of this civics class, Lyman argues that not everyone is bent on violence towards Americans, but most definitely all Americans are targets. The question, he insists, must be refined and made specific. So he writes his test question on the white board: 'Islamic extremist is to Islamic as — is to Christianity'; and provides his own answer: 'KKK.' 'That's what we're talking about – the [Klu Klux] Klan gone medieval and global. It could not have less to do with Islamic men and women of faith, of whom there are millions and millions' – including those in the American armed services, police and fire departments, he adds. The analogy, once made, is never explored, making it hard to see how it helps anyone to understand better the source and nature of the threat.

So the refined, specific question becomes: 'Why are Islamic extremists trying to kill us?' The question has one prime function, to explore what differentiates Us from Them, because the differences, everyone accepts, explain the motive force that unleashes terror. What defines America is what terrorists are against, which is the straightforward proposition on which all marshalling of information and discussion turns. For the students in the show, the difference between Us and Them is simply 'freedom and democracy'.

A great deal of the right-wing analysis of 9-11 was also pitched at this level. For example, in *The New York Observer*, columnist Richard Brookhiser suggested that the terrorists hate the fact that America is 'mighty and good'. 'The United States is perceived', Brookhiser wrote:

> correctly as the incarnation of a dominant world system – an empire of capitalism and democracy. New York City is also perceived as the hub of one of those subsystems, the roaring dynamo of wealth. Anyone in the world who looks at his lot and is unhappy, looks at us – country and city – and sees an alternative. If he has an aspiring frame of mind, he may try to come here or imitate us. If he has an aggrieved frame of mind, he will hold us responsible. If he has the resources of a hostile nation, or its functional equivalent, he will try to kill us ... The world's losers hate us because we are powerful, rich and good (or at least better than they are). When those who acted on that hatred have been repaid, seven times seven, we will rebuild the World Trade Towers, with one more story, just to rub it in.[2]

The theme of envy and jealousy figured strongly in much of the right-wing media. In the *Chicago Tribune*, Thomas Friedman, who coined the term 'They hate us' early in 2001, months before 9-11, laid the blame on 'pure envy'. 'Even in the club of industrialized democracies', he suggested, 'there is resentment at America's stature as the world's richest nation, its sole super-power, its predominant culture'.[3] The crux of the matter, declared Robert Kaplan, correspondent for *The Atlantic Monthly*, on National Public Radio (NPR), is 'a kind of existential hatred of a very dynamic, pulsing civilization, the West, challenging the middle classes of this part of the world and, therefore, a competitor to traditional Islam in a way that no other ideology has been'. Muslims are also anti-Communist, but, suggested Kaplan, they 'never really hated communism because it was such an abject, obvious failure'.[4] It's the success of American democracy and capitalism that is the real source of hatred.

The West Wing is above this kind of simplistic analysis. The show aimed, as it usually does, to be both urbane and worldly-wise, to champion such positive American values as open-mindedness, tolerance and the programme's favourite essential ethic, plurality. Lyman tells the students: 'It's probably a good idea to acknowledge that they do have specific complaints.' The 'complaints' that he itemises are: 'the people America supports'; 'US troops in Saudi Arabia'; 'sanctions against Iraq'; and 'support for Egypt'. And we are told that he hears these complaints every day. Since we can assume that the Deputy Chief of Staff is not in daily contact with terrorists or Islamic extremists, these cannot be the only people voicing these 'complaints'. In which case, it might be a suitable place to begin an instructive exploration of these issues, even if 'complaint' seems a distinctly neutral term for such contentious policy issues. It might, for example, be significant to consider the fact that such 'complaint' comes from many different sources – Americans, Europeans, people and governments across the Third World – as well as from Muslims. When such 'complaints' are made so often, from so many sources, might they not contribute to the creation of terrorism, or the conditions in which terrorism festers and recruits? But *The West Wing* finds such a question to be quite unnecessary. Lyman simply tells the class: 'I think they are wrong.' Therefore it need not detain our civics class from getting on with matters of real interest.

What explains terrorists, what defines their difference, is solely concerned with the nature and history of their beliefs – this is the essence of the lesson we are to be given. So what is Islamic extremism? 'It is strict adherence to a particular interpretation of seventh-century Islamic law, as practised by the Prophet Muhammad.' And Lyman adds for emphasis: 'When I say "strict adherence", I'm not kidding around.' With a single bound, at the very beginning of the civics lesson, we have been plunged into the sort of misinformation that is seriously detrimental to reasoned judgement. Islam was first preached by the Prophet Muhammad in the seventh century, in which case, by this definition, terrorism is original to Islam. If strict adherence to Islam 'as practised by the Prophet Muhammad' is what makes an extremist – and we have already been told that extremism has nothing to do with millions of Muslim men and women of faith – then what exactly is the connection between these many millions and their faith, or indeed the Prophet Muhammad? Presumably these millions are less than strict in their adherence. The practice of Prophet Muhammad is second only to the Qur'an itself and is essential for all Muslims, who refer to it as a guide and example of how to live; it provides the moral values and ethics of Islam, as well as such vital details as how to pray and what form prayer should take. Furthermore, all Islamic schools of law, which actually developed after the seventh century, as well as all shades of opinion and interpretation among all Muslims, are grounded in, refer to, and are justified by reasoning based on the practice of the Prophet Muhammad. So we are being offered a distinction that can only generate confusion and the inability to distinguish an Islamic extremist from any other Muslim.

Indeed, the liberal analysis of *The West Wing*, although couched in much more cautious and understanding language, turns out to be not far removed from the right-wing perspective on Islam and Muslims. The language of the right wing is hostile and uncompromising, as demonstrated by, for example, Karina Rollins, senior editor of *The American Enterprise*. 'It is a grave and dangerous mistake', she wrote, 'to leap from the fact that individual Muslims are innocent to the notion that the nations and societies in which they live are benign'. Islamic culture is intrinsically anti-West, innately full of hatred: 'There is no evidence that Muslims living in America are necessarily all great patriots.' President Bush's comments that 'Islam is not the enemy', while well-intended, were 'baseless assertions'. 'Islam is an imperialist religion'; and today 'this fresh enemy is at civilization's gate'.[5] *Newsweek* asked the hate question on its cover; and inside, recently appointed 'International Editor' Fareed Zakaria suggested that '[Muslims] come out of a culture that reinforces their hostility, distrust and hatred of the West – and of America in particular. This culture does not condone terrorism but fuels the fanaticism that is at its heart.'[6] In the conservative *Insight* magazine, Don Feder, syndicated columnist and editorial writer for the *Boston Herald*, proposed that President Bush's 'Disney version of Islam', which presents Islam as a peaceful religion, should be rejected by 'ordinary Americans'. Terrorism is not a 'deviation' but 'actually the norm' for Islamic culture:

> From its seventh-century breakout from the Arabian peninsula until the late 17th century, Islam advanced at sword point, spreading from the Pyrenees to the Philippines. The tide was checked only at the gates of Vienna. From the decline of the Ottoman Empire until the 1970s, Islam ebbed. Today – fuelled by oil wealth, surplus population, immigration and the rise of fundamentalism – Islam is resurgent. Instead of wild horsemen, its banners are carded by guerrillas, terrorists, theocrats and tyrants.[7]

The entire right-wing position was summed up rather neatly in a much reproduced and lengthy article by the military historian Victor Davis Hanson, which first appeared in the winter issue of *City Journal*. 'They hate us', he wrote, 'because their culture is backward and corrupt' and because 'they are envious of our power and prestige'. The general assumptions in left-wing and multicultural circles that 'there is some sort of equivalence – political, cultural and military – between the West and the Muslim world', or that 'America has been exceptionally unkind toward the Middle East', are false. For Hanson, democracy, consensual governance, constitution, freedom and citizenship are all European (Greek and Latin) inventions; they have nothing to do with the rest of the world in general, and the Muslim world in particular. Muslims are jealous of American success and superiority, 'which springs neither from luck nor resources, genes nor geography', but from its free market, free society, and, above all, its military might. There is an abyss between America and the world we actually live in: 'an abyss called power'. 'We should remember', notes Hanson, 'that the lethal, 2,500-year Western way of war is the reflection of very different ideas about personal freedom, civic militarism, individuality on the battlefield, military technology, logistics, decisive battle, group discipline, civilian audit and the dissemination and proliferation of knowledge'. It was Europeans, and not Ottomans, or Arabs, or Chinese, who 'colonized central and southern Africa, Asia and the Pacific and the Americas – and not merely because of their Atlantic ports or ocean ships but rather because of their longstanding attitudes and traditions about scientific inquiry, secular thought, free markets and individual ingenuity and spontaneity'. To sum up:

> We are militarily strong, and the Arab world abjectly weak, not because of greater courage, superior numbers, higher IQs, more ores or better weather, but because of our culture. When it comes to war, one billion people and the world's oil are not nearly as valuable military assets as MIT, West Point,

the House of Representatives, C-Span,[8] Bill O'Reilley and the G.I. Bill.[9] Between Xerxes on his peacock throne overlooking Salamis and Saddam on his balcony reviewing his troops, between the Greeks arguing and debating before they rowed out with Themistocles and the Americans haranguing one another on the eve of the Gulf War, lies a 2,500-year cultural tradition that explains why the rest of the world copies its weapons, uniforms and military organization from us, not vice versa.[10]

Of course, *The West Wing* could not be *that* coarse and jingoistic. But having defined the difference between Them and Us in terms supposedly original to the nature of Islam, it leaves us with few options. The show uses the Taliban to exemplify this difference: men forced to pray and grow their beards to a certain length, women denied education and employment and publicly stoned for crimes like not wearing a veil, the banning of films and television. The essence of the difference between Them and Us is lack of personal choice. 'There's nothing wrong with a religion whose laws say a man's got to wear a beard or cover his head or wear a collar. It's when violation of these laws becomes a crime against the state, and not your parents, that we are talking about lack of choice', we are informed. Furthermore, if the KKK provides a good religious analogy for Islamic extremists, there is also a political analogy. Here *The West Wing* quotes directly from a widely circulated letter written by the Afghan American, Tamim Ansary. The political analogy for the Taliban is the Nazis, and the people of Afghanistan are the Jews in the concentration camps. Opposing the Nazis was a good thing, so by analogy, a war against the Taliban must be equally justified.

A number of left-wing writers also picked up this point. Most notably, journalist Christopher Hitchens paraded this assertion with mindless banality. However, the analogy is not only a little too convenient but also totally absurd. For one thing, the Taliban were not racists – indeed, racial equality was a basic tenet of their outlook. They had a puritan ideology, certainly, but it was hardly based on any coherent philosophy, let alone something as elaborate as the Third Reich. They produced neither a Heidegger nor a Wagner. While the Taliban were an extremely repressive regime, they did not practise ethnic cleansing or genocide, nor did they produce gas chambers. Their repression was directed solely at their own people. Nor were they bent on world domination – even though they allowed bin Laden to flourish among them, and he probably did harbour such desires. You don't become a Nazi simply because you reject the modern world, or force your population to practise a strict code of conduct, or behave generally in a chauvinist manner. The Nazi analogy accomplished only one thing – to suppress relevant questions. Where did the Taliban come from? What were the circumstances and background that led the Taliban to overthrow the previous government of Afghanistan? Why did the Taliban's own religious scholars so overwhelmingly condemn the attacks on America as contrary to Islamic law?

However, if the Taliban stand for all Islamic extremists, then by analogy all Islamic extremists are terrorists. Which leads the students gathered in the virtual universe of *The West Wing* to the next question: what was the first act of terrorism? We are told that a secret cult led by the fanatical Mullah, Hasan ibn al-Sabah, committed the first act of terrorism in the eleventh century. Al-Sabah's followers, who were taught to believe in nothing and dare all, carried out swift and treacherous murders of fellow Muslims and did so in a state of religious ecstasy induced by hashish and with the promise of Paradise. So not only is extremism original to Islam, but the first terrorists were Muslims who preyed upon Muslims. The history of the world before the eleventh century then becomes devoid of any kind of terrorism! What this piece of potted history also leaves out is the fact that the *hashshashin*, from which comes the word 'assassin', arose in the context of the Crusades; they were employed as much by the Crusaders as by various Muslim groups jostling for power. It is one thing to use the antics of the Old Man of the Mountain, as al-Sabah was known, to understand and locate the nefarious activities of bin Laden. It is quite another to suggest that Muslim history is the origin and prime source of assassins and terrorists. And an assassin is not a terrorist; there is a distinction between the terms and the actions they imply. The assassins committed individual acts of political murder: their targets were kings and viziers with whom they had a particular grievance. The term 'terrorists' was first coined by Edmund Burke to refer to those who conducted The Terror, the bloody, guillotine-wielding phase of that campaign for liberty, equality and fraternity known as the French Revolution. Assassination is politically motivated murder directed at specific individuals, and is not designed to kill innocent bystanders. Terrorism is politically motivated aggression, warfare, that defines whole classes of people or nations as enemies who are collectively responsible and guilty. Where no one is innocent, everyone is a potential target by design, though not necessarily by intent in each specific instance.

These are, of course, distinctions too subtle not just for a television show but also for the standard analysis presented by the left and right. In *The West Wing*'s discussion of terrorism, Sam Seaborn, introduced to the class as the resident White House expert on the subject, is asked what strikes him most about terrorism. 'Its 100% failure rate', he replies without hesitation. This was perhaps intended as a reassurance for a worried public, but it hardly passes muster as an examination of the history of terrorism. The complete failure rate of terrorism comes about, says Seaborn, because: (1) terrorists 'always fail in what they are after'; and (2) 'they pretty much always succeed in strengthening whatever it is they're against'. Not even a group of high school children can fail to demur at this. What about the IRA? Well, says Sam, the Brits and the Protestants are still there. This is hardly a precise reflection of the political objectives of the IRA. It forgets that 'Brits out' is now, and has long been, an accepted proposition that will be determined by the votes of Protestants and Catholics. Nor does it recognise the complex story of the rise of Sinn Fein, who have just taken up their parliamentary offices in Westminster, the home of the British Parliament. The Basque extremists have had no results, says Seaborn. Again, this ignores the considerable accommodations that Spain has made in granting greater autonomy to the Basque region. And 'the Red Brigades, Baader-Meinhof and the Weathermen sought to overthrow capitalism and capitalism's doing fine'. Well, true enough, but unquiet lies the theory that wears the crown, and the criticisms of capitalism have not gone away. (The programme was made, of course, before the latest upsurge of violence by the Red Brigades in Italy.) Each of these assertions is open to serious question, as is the purpose for which political violence was used in each historical context by these different groups. *The West Wing* sidesteps completely any consideration that, ultimately, campaigns of terrorism lead to a political process of negotiation, accommodation and *rapprochement*, and result in change.

Seamlessly, the discussion moves to the question of non-violent protest, which presumably is a related subject, although the nature of the relationship is worth more discussion and thought than simply lumping everything in one pot. More than anything else in the aftermath of 9-11, this is a relationship that we have to clarify. We need to consider the distinctions between people and groups with similar – or even the same – objectives that nevertheless generate different campaigns, different policies and different kinds of mobilisation. *The West Wing* simply assures us that non-violent protest worked for Gandhi and the civil rights movement. So terrorism, in this view, is many things – a broad enough term to bracket everything from the unmentioned al-Qaeda to Gandhi and the American revolutionaries at the Boston Tea Party (who we are told declared war most court-eously), and still warrant the judgement that it always fails.

We now move on to the awkward choices that terrorism presents to society: the balance between liberty and safety. One of the students quotes Benjamin Franklin's aphorism: 'They that can give up essential liberty to obtain a little temporary safety deserve neither liberty nor safety.' *The West Wing* offers a strident defence of the national security state, presented by C.J. Cregg, White House Press Secretary. The liberal objections are voiced by Toby Ziegler, the Communications Director. The essence of the discussion is to convince the students that human spies are needed, phone tapping may be required, and certain cherished liberties may have to be compromised if the citizens of America are to feel safe. The reality of terrorism presents a clear and present danger, and to combat it effectively America needs partners who may not be great believers in freedom and democracy, or that much different from the Taliban. And, C.J. admits, this agenda has consequences for free speech and doesn't begin to wrestle with the problem of people being 'lynched by the patriotism police for voicing an opinion'. Nevertheless, she insists, we need to acknowledge that covert actions of the CIA variety are not only necessary and expedient, but their success and effectiveness speaks for itself. C.J. lists the triumphs of the recent past: the Soviets never crossed the Elbe, the North Koreans stayed behind the 38th parallel and the millennium passed off peacefully. For all the inherent risks to liberty, such as blacklists, McCarthy-type witch-hunts and unlawful detentions, safety owes a debt to the sort of remedies currently needed to defeat terrorists. If all this sounds too strident, C.J. tells the students: 'Nothing is more American than coalition building. The first thing John Wayne always did was put together a posse.' So, for *The West Wing*, which displays its immaculate liberal credentials at every opportunity, posse law, covert operations, US interventions (military and otherwise) and much else besides is justifiable in the name of safety and the American way. The show does not raise the question that these activities may be one of the 'specific complaints' of all those who 'hate us'.

But for Chalmers Johnson, a retired cold warrior now teaching at the University of California, there is little doubt of this. It is precisely these elements of American foreign policy that have generated the hatred of, and terrorism against, the United States. On NPR's 'All Things Considered', in analysing what had occurred, Johnson used the term 'blowback', coined by the CIA in the 1950s to refer to unintended consequences of covert operations that come back to haunt the United States. When the term was first used, it referred to the consequences of the CIA's assassination of the then Iranian Prime Minister, Muhammad Mussadegh. 'The result of this egregious interference in the affairs of Iran was to bring the Shah to power and 25 years of repression and tyranny, leading finally to the holding of the entire US Embassy in Tehran hostage for over a year and the revolution of the Ayatollah Khomeini', said Johnson. The perpetual expansion of the 'American empire' and its 'overextended reach', he argued, was the root cause of 'Nine Eleven'.[11] Similar sentiments were expressed by Noam Chomsky, Professor of Linguistics at MIT and lifelong dissident. Chomsky dismissed the 'fashionable' excuses offered both by the right and the left. 'Such excuses are convenient for the US and much of the West', he told a radio station in Belgrade. 'To quote the lead analysis in the *New York Times* [16 September]: "the perpetrators acted out of hatred for the values cherished in the West as freedom, tolerance, prosperity, religious pluralism and universal suffrage". US actions are irrelevant, and therefore need not even be mentioned. This is a comforting picture', but 'it happens to be completely at variance with everything we know, but has all the merits of self-adulation and uncritical support for power'.[12] Elsewhere, Chomsky asked Americans to 'recognize that in much of the world the US is regarded as a leading terrorist state, and with good reason. We might bear in mind, for example, that in 1986 the US was condemned by the World Court for "unlawful use of force" (international terrorism) and then vetoed a Security Council resolution calling of all states (meaning the US) to adhere to international law.'[13]

The West Wing's definition of terrorism is much simpler: it's a product of intolerance motivated by inability to accept the programme's trademark recipe for all problems – pluralism. Pluralism, then, by its very nature is a threat to the existence of all those who strictly adhere to a system of law and practice that permits no deviation, that imposes totalitarian compliance. Those who adhere to these rigid systems are threatened not merely by the multicultural nature of American society, the existence of different faiths, races and ways of life openly practised side by side, but also by the ability to entertain a plurality of ideas on any given subject. Once again, stereotype overlays history and crowds out necessary information which it should be essential for an under-informed public to consider. The history of Muslim society and Islam as religion and law is founded on the toleration of plurality. Islam is intrinsically a pluralistic world-view, as much of its history illustrates so vividly. Moorish Spain, Spain under the rule of Muslims, was the golden age of Jewish Talmudic scholarship. When Spain was reconquered by the Most Catholic monarchs, Ferdinand and Isabella, the ethos of national racial purity required the expulsion of the Jews, who sought refuge in, and were embraced with open arms by, the Muslim Ottoman Empire. Pluralism, far from being an exclusive development of modern society, also has a history. But this need not disturb the assurance of the civics class being conducted in the special episode of *The West Wing*.

The show does acknowledge that there is a problem in being a Muslim. This is demonstrated in the sub-plot, the questioning of Raqim Ali. This White House staffer with the same name as a wanted terrorist is an Arab American MIT graduate. He is bundled into an office, where he must answer for his father making a contribution to something called the Holy Land Defender, and for his participation in demonstrations protesting against the presence of American troops in Saudi Arabia. Ali explains that Saudi Arabia is home to Islam's two holiest sites, and that for him the real objective of American military intervention was protecting America's oil interest. But most of all, he objects to the double standards by which an army composed of women as well as men was sent 'to protect a Muslim dynasty where women aren't even allowed to drive a car!' Ali's objections prompt an immediate paternalist defence of American foreign policy from Leo McGarry, the exceptionally nice Chief of Staff. 'Maybe we can teach 'em', he says. For all its liberal credentials, this sub-plot is unapologetic, explicit and emotive. Ali says that it's not uncommon for Arab Americans to be the first suspected 'when this kind of thing happens', and it's simply 'horrible'. Speaking for the masses, nice Leo retorts: 'I can't imagine why. No! I'm trying to figure out why anytime there's terrorist activity people always assume its Arabs.' Then he works himself up to the clincher: 'It's the price you pay.' So there we have it. Being a Muslim has a price tag: an emotive ignorance that confuses Arab with Muslim, Middle East with terror (even though according to a 1997 Report by the State Department, terrorism originating from the Middle East is sixth in order of frequency), politics with religion, to generate the rationale for a scenario in which there is a real enemy within. Presumably, Ali must pay the same price as Japanese Americans who had the misfortune to have the face of the enemy during World War II and therefore could be interned and stripped of their property and livelihood for national security. The sub-plot is abruptly terminated when the other Raqim Ali, the real suspect, is located in Germany, leaving the protagonist of these scenes – the nice, humane Leo – to contemplate what he has said.

But what Leo says is not acceptable to all Americans. Is being a Muslim American any different from being, say, an Irish or Italian American? Should Muslims pay a price simply for being Muslims? Does equality apply only to certain kinds of Americans? Dennis Kucinich, Democratic Congressman from Cleveland, Ohio, and veteran defender of free speech and civil liberties, had no doubts. Delivering his speech to the Southern California Americans for Democratic Action in Los Angeles in the form of a prayer, Kucinich began with the declaration that there is a deeper truth expressed in the unity of the United States. That implicit in the union of our country is the union of all people. That all people are essentially one. That the world is interconnected not only on the material level of economics, trade, communication, and transportation, but innerconnected through human consciousness, through the human heart, through the heart of the world, through the simply expressed impulse and yearning to be and to breathe free. I offer this prayer for America.

In sharp contrast to *The West Wing*'s assertion that the activities of the CIA and FBI are necessary for preserving liberty and democracy, Kucinich suggested that giving free rein to such organisations undermines the very basis of the American constitution and the ideas of liberty and democracy. He prayed that America would not be trapped in a 'siege mentality', in 'the Patriot Games, the Mind Games, the War Games of an unelected President and his unelected Vice President'. He prayed that America would not put aside 'guarantees of constitutional justice', cancel the First Amendment (the right of free speech, the right to assemble peaceably), the Fourth Amendment (the prohibitions against unreasonable search and seizure), the Fifth Amendment (which prohibits indefinite incarceration without trial), the Sixth Amendment (the right to prompt and public trial), and the Eighth Amendment (which protects against cruel and unusual punishment). He prayed that America would listen to the voice of the people, and itemised a selection of actions taken in their name but without their direct approval or consent:

Because we did not authorize the invasion of Iraq.
We did not authorize the invasion of Iran.
We did not authorize the invasion of North Korea.
We did not authorize the bombing of civilians in Afghanistan.

We did not authorize permanent detainees in Guantanamo Bay.

We did not authorize the withdrawal from the Geneva Convention.

We did not authorize military tribunals suspending due process and habeas corpus.

We did not authorize assassination squads.

We did not authorize the resurrection of COINTELPRO.[14]

We did not authorize the repeal of the Bill of Rights.

We did not authorize the revocation of the Constitution.

We did not authorize national identity cards.

We did not authorize the eye of Big Brother to peer from cameras throughout our cities.

We did not authorize an eye for an eye.

Nor did we ask that the blood of innocent people, who perished on September 11, be avenged with the blood of innocent villagers in Afghanistan.

We did not authorize the administration to wage war anytime, anywhere, anyhow it pleases.

We did not authorize war without end.

We did not authorize a permanent war economy.[15]

The West Wing, much like many of the foaming-at-the-mouth pundits and commentators, unreservedly declines to think of America's own history, as well as the history of its interaction with the world during the last five decades. After 9-11, this history was uppermost in the minds of left-wing writers and thinkers, many of whom took exception to America automatically assuming a moral high ground. Much of this criticism was notable for its sheer tartness. For example, in the literary fortnightly, the *London Review of Books*, a constellation of regular contributors announced that America deserves to be hated. In a much-criticised piece, Mary Beard, lecturer in classics at Cambridge University, stated simply: 'the United States had it coming'. 'World bullies, even if their heart is in the right place, will

in the end pay the price', she said.[16] Indian novelist and critic
Amit Chaudhuri compared various American governments to
the former Indian Prime Minister, Mrs Indira Gandhi. Mrs
Gandhi pretended to be democratic, freedom-loving and secular-
ist, while she used every undemocratic means, suppressed every
freedom and inflamed religious fires to perpetuate her own and
her party's rule and dominance. She meddled with India's feder-
alist structure, destabilised states governed by opposition parties, and used Sikhs, Hindus and Muslims against each other to
further her aims. In particular, she supported and promoted the
Sikh fundamentalists, Jarnail Singh Bhindranwale and his Akali
Dal party. When Bhindranwale turned against Mrs Gandhi and
sought refuge in the Golden Temple in Amritsar, she used the
army to attack the Temple and kill him. The aftermath was hardly
surprising: Mrs Gandhi was assassinated by her Sikh body-
guard; and thugs from her party murdered countless innocent
Sikhs in Delhi. 'Like Mrs Gandhi in India', writes Chaudhuri,

> America has been a great, self-appointed proponent of demo-
> cracy in the modern world, while, in actuality, it has treated it
> as a nuisance and an obstruction when it gets in the way of
> its self-interest. It now justifies war by speaking of the 'will of
> the people' but the will of the people in Palestine has, for
> decades, meant little more than the rubble of Palestine. In order
> to root out Communism from Afghanistan, it armed a reli-
> gious extremist group; and created, in effect, a Bhindranwale.
> For years, America's foreign policy, like Mrs Gandhi's dom-
> estic policy, has been concerned solely with extending its own
> sphere of influence, whatever the cost. Only the American
> public can put pressure on, and change, the aberrant policy:
> but the American public's main source of information about
> its country's foreign policy is Hollywood with its images of
> terror and frightening rhetoric of 'good' and 'evil'.[17]

According to novelist Doris Lessing, America is a country in which 'everything is taken to extremes'. In her contribution to *Granta* magazine's forum on 'What we think of America', Lessing pointed out that 'the reaction to the events of 11 September – terrible as they were – seems excessive to outsiders, and we have to say this to our American friends, although they have become so touchy, and ready to break off relations with accusations of hard-heartedness'. She defended Mary Beard's comments by suggesting that 'the judgement "they had it coming", so angrily resented, is perhaps misunderstood. What people felt was that Americans had at last learned that they are like everyone else, vulnerable to the snakes of Envy and Revenge, to bombs exploding on a street corner (as in Belfast), or in a hotel housing a government (as in Brighton). They say themselves that they have been expelled from their Eden. How strange they should ever have thought they had a right to one.' Gripped by patriotic fever, Americans see themselves 'as unique, alone, misunderstood, beleaguered, and they see any criticism as treachery'.[18] Harold Pinter, celebrated playwright and actor, was even more scathing. The US has 'exercised sustained, systematic, remorseless and quite clinical manipulation of power worldwide, while masquerading as a force for universal good', he wrote. It is 'arrogant, indifferent, contemptuous of International Law, both dismissive and manipulative of the United Nations: this is now the most dangerous power the world has ever known – the authentic "rogue state", but a "rogue state" of colossal military and economic might'. But the world has had enough of America. Now, there is 'a profound revulsion and disgust with the manifestation of US power and global capitalism which is growing throughout the world and becoming a formidable force in its own right'.[19]

Of course, all this was not going to go unchallenged. The very idea that the US is reaping the fruits of imperialism was attacked by many commentators as a position that condones evil. Joe Klein, author of *Primary Colors* and Washington correspondent of *The New Yorker*, dismissed it simply as 'morally bankrupt carping'.[20] And most of those who criticised America and its foreign policy were treated in a fashion not too far removed from the treatment of Raqim Ali in *The West Wing*. As *The Guardian* reported:

> Within days of the deaths in New York and Washington, anyone, it seemed, who had ever been publicly critical of America or globalisation suddenly found themselves accused of complicity with Osama bin Laden – and worse. In the British press alone, they have been described as 'defeatist' and 'unpatriotic', 'nihilist' and 'masochistic', and both 'Stalinist' and 'fascist'; as 'Baader Meinhof gang', 'the hand-maidens of Osama' and 'an auxiliary to dictators'; as 'limp', 'wobbly', 'heartless and stupid'; and 'worm eaten by Soviet propaganda'; as full of 'loose talk', 'wilful self-delusion' and 'intellectual decadence'; as a collection of 'useful idiots', 'dead-eyed zombies'; and 'people who hate people'.[21]

Cosmic events, such as 9-11, do not allow you to be neutral. And one should not be too surprised at the torrent of abuse for taking an unpalatable position. But cosmic events also beg for cosmic conclusions. In the closing segments of *The West Wing*, the civics class asks its final question: how did all this start? By now, the First Lady has appeared in the Mess and it falls on her to come up with an answer; and the answer provides the title for this special episode: 'Isaac and Ishmael'. According to the First Lady, the problem begins with the Biblical story of Abraham and his sons. 'And so it began: the Jews, the sons of Isaac. The Arabs, the sons of Ishmael.' In which case, the attack on America is understood to be directly connected to the question of Israel, and the question of Israel is explained by a dispute with Biblical origins, a dispute that has stood through time to wreak havoc and disaster. If the dispute – far from being a ter-ritorial feud – is of Biblical origins and Biblical proportions, then it can hardly have a real political or policy-based solution.

There is little that we – as individuals, Americans, people of the world – can do about it. The course suggested by Canadian Justice Minister, Anne McLennan – 'we have to honestly assess why we believe this is happening' and, if 'there is any necessity', to change our 'policy or approaches' – becomes redundant.[22] There is no necessity to change. When all is said and done, *The West Wing* refuses to confront the real issue and prefers to cop out.

The show ends with a final exhortation to the departing students to keep on entertaining more than one thought. The trouble is, thought without *information* does not advance understanding. It is the quality and accuracy of information, coupled with original thought, that produces understanding, unlocks meaning and provides potential answers to difficult problems. The sensibilities of *The West Wing* and its prescription for treating the problem of terrorism are, as usual, a tribute to the best of American values. The information at its disposal is the insurmountable flaw that makes it resort to disinformation, obfuscation and gross stereotype, the perfect mirror of opinion, comment and expertise in the parallel universe that is the real world.

The 'Isaac and Ishmael' special episode of *The West Wing* was introduced by the regular cast members. They appealed to the audience to donate money to the victims of 9-11; profits from the programme were also donated to this cause. The reaction to the episode was as polarised as the opinions of the right and the left on the causes of 9-11 and the vexing question that the fateful events of that day raised: 'Why do people hate America?' On one side, there was support for a creative attempt to provide an exploration of the issues; on the other, condemnation for hubris, smug pedantry, preachiness and overweening self-importance. The point, however, is that this was not 'just television'. The logic and illogic, arguments and obfuscation, rationale and justification, history lessons and analysis provided by *The West Wing* followed the same footsteps as all of the news coverage, commentary, analysis and debate in the real world. In this instance, the parallel reality was a mirror; what it mirrored were the premises and entrenched positions constructed out of the question of why people feel hatred for America. What this virtual reflection makes clear is that the terms of debate are seen through a glass darkly, blurred, misshapen and imprecise. *The West Wing* has fared no better or worse than politicians, experts and hosts of journalists. What it has presented most effectively, if we are prepared to be open-minded, is how far we need to go beyond a single question to make sense of what has happened, how response has proceeded and should proceed, and where security and resolution can be found. So far, the question of people's hostility to America has been leading the analysis. Perhaps we ought to look at the question itself and see what assumptions lie beneath it.

CHAPTER TWO

'They' 'Evil', 'Hate' 'America'

From the first televised statement and State of the Union address by the real President, to television's virtual White House in *The West Wing*, in acres of news coverage, comment and opinion on television and in print, the question 'Why do people hate America?' has been endlessly repeated. The phrase has taken on the character of a proposition, an accepted premise from which discussion begins. But as a question, the phrase marshals terms that have meaning and implications far beyond the events of 9-11. It is not just an emotive question asked in the heat of the moment – it is a question that uses emotive terms to place the heat of the moment in a much broader context, a context of events and ideas before and after 9-11.

If a question is a search for more information and ideas than are on offer, then we need to start by understanding the terms of the question. The question 'Why do people hate America?' has three basic components: 'people', hatred, America.

Who are these people? How are individuals or groups assigned to this category – what characterises them? The 'people' are defined by the quality assigned to them: hatred. Hatred puts people on the defensive and makes them ready to attack as well as defend. And it has a history; it is too often a motive force in human affairs. Hatred defines boundaries between peoples, creates the distance, distrust and animosity that makes it possible to commit heinous crimes. Hatred provides a context, a set of conventions that are understood. But do these conventions explain why America is a target?

Hatred is a resentment that always evokes a response. It creates a set of mutual perceptions between those people who hate and the subject of their hatred. It is, history suggests, as dangerous to consider oneself the subject of hatred, to fear the onslaught of other people's hatred, as to hold others as the object of hatred. Between the 'people' that the question seeks to identify and 'America' there is not one line of explanation but a mutual relationship that has to be unfolded, understood, evaluated and resolved.

Finally, the question comes to America. What is the America that is hated, and how is it related to the America that is loved, the America understood by those who seek to identify the perpetrators of hatred? So, a simple impassioned question makes assumptions about some of the most complex issues; and that's why we have to interrogate the question rather than be bamboozled into ready-packaged, easy answers.

On the morning of 9-11, as the world watched in horror, there was no doubt about the identity of the people responsible. The first thought in everyone's mind was simple: the terrorists were Muslim/Arab/Islamic/extremists/fundamentalists; they were the 'people', it was 'Them'. The conclusion came before investigation or evidence because it is a generic idea, a convention, a cultural cliché, the easiest assumption to which we have been preconditioned. How does this predisposition, this ready-made suspicion, affect the response to 9-11? Does it complicate the issue, or make it easier? Indeed, does it assist in identifying the specific perpetrators of those crimes and tracking them down, or does it blur the distinctive nature of the crime and the criminals responsible by pointing to an undifferentiated general class, 'people', who are part and parcel of the circumstances that made this crime possible? These questions raise a broader context: a history of ideas, knowledge and cultural conventions. It is this broader cultural context that we must examine.

The terrorist actions challenged our credulity in only one sense – this was real and not a Hollywood screenplay. How far do the imaginary scenarios of innumerable films and novels provide the context in which we understand this real crime and the question it produced? Nothing in the Hollywood archives desensitised anyone to the shock and horror of 9-11. But it is far less easy to determine how responses to those events have been clouded by make-believe pictures, the movies we have seen. The top box-office attraction for two weeks in April 2000 was *Rules of Engagement*, a film described by ADC, the American–Arab Anti-Discrimination Committee, as 'probably the most vicious anti-Arab racist film ever made by a major Hollywood studio'. Paramount Pictures responded by arguing that the film was 'a fictional account of the consequences of extremism in all its forms', insisting that it was 'not an indictment of any government, culture, or people'. Yet in his review for the website Film.com, Peter Brunette reported that 'the audience I saw the film with cheered when the Marines slaughtered the civilians'.[1]

Rules of Engagement is a film that turns on perceptions of events and people, specifically one horrific event that we are repeatedly asked to look at in closer detail until the film-makers are satisfied that we have seen what should be known. The central event of the film takes place in Yemen, where the US embassy is under siege from protesters. A detachment of Marines is despatched from a nearby aircraft carrier to strengthen security, and if events warrant to evacuate embassy personnel. As the helicopters fly in, armed gunmen have taken up positions on nearby rooftops and are firing on the Embassy. In the square below, the protesters are still gathered, shouting, waving fists and throwing rocks at the building. The Marines enter the compound and are pinned down on the rooftop by sniper fire. Once the Ambassador and his family have been evacuated, the Marines take casualties and the officer in command issues the order to open fire, not on the snipers but on the crowd. The Marines mow down men, women and children. This is the point at which the audience cheered, according to Brunette. When the Marines cease firing, the scene goes quiet and we see that no one is left standing in the square below – a scene of carnage, with 83 dead and hundreds wounded.

The narrative of the film then becomes a courtroom drama. Charges of murder, conduct unbecoming and breach of the peace are brought against the Marine colonel who ordered the slaughter. As the trial unfolds we get to see the bloody fire-fight a number of times from various vantage points, each adding more detail, until eventually all is revealed. What do we learn of the people who at the outset are presented as innocent civilian victims? These people are not characters, they are a crowd. We learn that they demonstrate on a weekly basis outside the US Embassy. What motivates these demonstrations? Copies of tape cassettes are found lying around in the ruined embassy, even beside the beds of the mortally wounded languishing in hospital. In the court, the tapes are translated. We learn that they contain a declaration of 'Islamic jihad against the United States' and call for all Americans, civilian or military, to be killed. So much for motivation. What effect do these tapes have on our perception of events in the crowd?

The second time we revisit the scenes outside the embassy, the people have become willing dupes among whom armed gunmen can operate with impunity. The crowd do not disperse at the sound of gunfire – they intensify their protest. The gunmen on the rooftops are shown taking up position in front of women in chadors; one of the women stands there holding a child in her arms. The third revision shows, contrary to evidence given by the doctor who tends the wounded, that there are also gunmen in the crowd of demonstrators. The final revision reveals that everyone in the crowd is armed – men, women who bring weapons from under their black robes, and children – they all open fire on the Marines, even the emotive figure of the one-legged little girl who, in several scenes, has been seen hobbling around on crutches. The crippled child, with her sweet face and doe eyes, turns into a demon-eyed assassin aiming a gun at heavily-armed American soldiers.

What the courtroom drama establishes is that the Marine colonel correctly assessed the situation. He is exonerated. The politicians and diplomats are shown to have lied, obstructed justice, and tried to operate a cover-up. Before the credits roll, we get a series of captions, a standard device of all those 'based on a true story' movies. The captions update the audience on the fate of the characters after the events portrayed in the movie. In this instance, we are told that the National Security Adviser and the Ambassador got their come-uppance. The film deliberately presents its narrative as occurring in America's recent history, which led the Yemeni Ambassador to the US, Abdel-Wahab Al Hajjri, to note that many viewers were asking: 'When did this happen?'[2]

The Pentagon participated in the making of this film, as it so often does with movies depicting the military. When complaints were made, Pentagon spokesman Kenneth Bacon explained that his department's primary concern was that 'movies provide a fair and, hopefully accurate, portrayal of the military'. Beyond that specific concern, studios 'have a right to make the movies any way they want to make them'.[3] But who scrutinises and advises on how the 'people', the crowd of adversaries, are represented? 'All of a sudden Yemenis, even women and children, have become terrorists, and they want to kill Americans. This is outrageous', Yemeni Ambassador Al-Hajjri protested.[4] Jack Shaheen, author of the book *The TV Arab*, told the Middle East newspaper *Al Ahram Weekly* that he considered the film 'the worst ever'. It conveys a simple message: 'It is appropriate and morally correct to kill Arabs, even children.' Hollywood, he added, finds it 'perfectly acceptable to vilify, to demonise whatever and whoever is Arab and Muslim'.[5] His view was reinforced by former US Ambassador to Yemen, William Rugh, now president of AMID-

EAST, an organisation working to promote greater understanding of the Middle East among Americans. Rugh is reported as saying: 'It is a biased film that reinforces prejudice against Arabs'; he added that the film's 'misrepresentation' was a product of ignorance.[6]

What does cinema, popular entertainment, have to do with a question – 'Why do they hate us?' – posed in the midst of the most harrowing reality? Popular culture and its conventions form part of the context and circumstances, the ideas and information, in which the question is framed and answers are offered. The 'people' that the question seeks to understand are enveloped in a cultural cliché. These 'people' are a generality, a backdrop against which innumerable stories – with troubling parallels to the now real horror – have been told. The conventions of storytelling have kept on blurring the difference between the mass of the 'people' and the specific adversary, the terrorist. The more *Rules of Engagement* probes the perceptions of its central event, the more it reiterates the thesis of so many other Hollywood films of recent times, such as *Iron Eagle*, *True Lies* and *The Siege*, in which 'Islamic terrorism' is the plot device, the hook on which a thriller or action picture is suspended. It is not just the terrorist who has become a stock character, a one-dimensional figure whose only function is to be fanatical and plot mayhem and death to Americans. The 'people', the generality of ordinary people from among whom terrorists come, are represented as sharing the same characteristics as those who commit acts of terror. In such films as *Delta Force*, in which Palestinian terrorists take over a plane, and *The Harem*, in which an Arab prince goes out of his way to enslave white people, guilt is not simply associated with the individuals involved but is transferred to all Palestinians, Arabs and Muslims in general.

In the 1996 film *Executive Decision*, a group of Islamic fundamentalist terrorists hijack a passenger airliner to transport a chemical weapon into the US. The executive decision of the title is the Presidential order to shoot down the passenger jet, an order put in operation after 9-11. In the 1998 film *The Siege*, a series of devastating bomb attacks on New York leads to the creation of internment camps for Arab and Muslim Americans. After 9-11, we have had the Patriot Act (introduced on 26 October 2001, which merges the functions of intelligence agencies and domestic law enforcement, giving them sweeping new powers and thus eliminating the checks and balances that previously gave courts the opportunity to ensure that these powers were not abused), an estimated 1,200 people have been detained without access to lawyers, and there is a prison camp at Guantanamo Bay in Cuba where prisoners are being held whose exact legal status is unclear. The films we have seen provide a context for all of these real events. Should we not examine how far the fictional stereotypes fill in what most people the world over do not know or understand about the facts in real life?

Spectacular cinematic devastation pales into insignificance in contrast to the events of 9-11. But there is no corresponding diminution in the link between the atmosphere of real fear, threat and present danger and its cinematic representations. Real fear can use the emotive landscape of cinema to provide reasons. The cinema gives faces to the faceless 'people', the generic crowd, and projects one insistent idea of what motivates 'Them': hatred.

Hatred has always used stereotypes to justify hostility and aggression, to explain why the most basic rights of one people can be denied or violated by another group. Stereotypes make hating easy. Popular culture throughout history has produced the material in which stereotypes are most in evidence, and which have been most effective in stimulating and sustaining hatred. For example, the pernicious and false blood libel against the Jews lurked in the popular imagination of Europe for centuries, and 'Shylock', the name of Shakespeare's Jewish character, has become a slang term for all unscrupulous money-lenders and loan sharks. The Nazis made films playing on all these old stereotypes as the backdrop for representing Jews as rats infesting

German cities. Popular culture does not make the political parties, the legislation, the armies that fight to sustain and defend racism, but it has always been their best recruiting agent. The movies embroider, distil and concentrate, but what they present is actually out there.

But stereotypes have a strong presence on both sides of the divide – among those who hate and those who claim to be hated. Consider the leaflet distributed around the mosques of Britain by the extremist group Hizb ut-Tahrir, a few weeks after 9-11. Under the title 'The Campaign to Subvert Islam as an Ideology and a System', the leaflet announces that America has declared a 'Crusade against Islam and Muslims'. The 'unbelievers' are jealous of Muslim unity and envious of the power of Islam. America mocks and scorns Islam at every opportunity, 'humiliates her sincere sons, corrupts her societies, plunders her treasures, kills the innocent and challenges the Muslims day and night in their belief. While the Crusades of the past were aimed at occupying parts of the Islamic lands, today's Crusade launched against Islam and Muslims aims to subvert Islam by making Muslims reject their creed and embrace the creed of secularism.' The leaflet urges Muslims to accept 'the correct Islamic view': 'that Islam is the Haqq [Truth] – everything other than Islam is batil [falsehood]'; and to fight Americans. All Muslims are duty bound, it states, to fight the unbelievers, since God has 'laid down the clear foundation of the relationship between Islam and other religions and doctrines. This foundation is that Islam and Kufr [unbelief] will never mix under any circumstances whatsoever.' The only solution is jihad, which is to be understood purely as 'Qitaal' (fighting).[7] Such religiously motivated hatred is not unique to Hizb ut-Tahrir – it can be found in the pronouncements of many fundamentalists and extremist groups in the Middle East, Pakistan and South-East Asia.

But such sentiments have mirror images. After his newspaper took an anti-bombing stance, Khaled al-Maeena, the editor-in-chief of the English-language Saudi paper *Arab News*, received an avalanche of e-mails from America. A reader in Montana wrote on 15 December 2001: 'I hate you all. The Koran is the book of Satan, the devil, the teachings of evil, the book that is used to justify murder. Anyone who worships Islam is the devil's child. There will be a great conflict in the future, a conflagration between Islam and Christianity, and the crusaders of Christianity will rid the world of the Satanic hell that is Islam ...' Another reader named Tom wrote on 29 January 2002: 'I'm an American. I can't wait until we are no longer in need of Saudi oil so we will not have to deal with you crazies anymore. The world would be a much more peaceful place if all you religious zealots would just go away.' Al-Maeena, an unabashed America-lover who studied in the US and sent four of his five children to American colleges, chose not to ignore but to engage with his correspondents. Slowly, through deliberate use of moderation and a number of exchanges, he was able to appease his correspondents and take them beyond stereotypes.[8]

Hatred festers in isolation. And sometimes – but not always – it can be transcended through engagement. Chris Toensing, the highly respected editor of the *Middle East Report*, describes a 1998 encounter with a waiter whom he met in the quiet Egyptian port of Suez. 'As I sipped tea in his café', writes Toensing,

> he pulled up a chair to chat, as Egyptians often do to welcome strangers. Not long into our amiable repartee, he looked me in the eye. 'Now I want to ask you a blunt question', he said. 'Why do you Americans hate us?' I raised my eyebrows, so he explained what he meant and, in doing so, provided some insights into why others hate us.
>
> Numerous United Nations resolutions clearly define Israel's occupation of the West Bank, Gaza Strip, and East Jerusalem as illegal. Yet Israel receives 40 percent of all US foreign aid, more the [sic] United States' annual foreign aid total, more than $3.5 billion annually in recent years, roughly $500 per Israeli citizen. (The average Egyptian will earn $656 this

year). Israel uses all of this aid money to build new settlements on Palestinian land and to buy US-made warplanes and helicopter gunships. 'Why do Americans support Israel when Israel represses Arabs?' the waiter asked. He went on: Evidence clearly shows that the US-led economic sanctions on Iraq punish Iraqi civilians while hardly touching Saddam Hussein's regime. A UNICEF study in 1999 backed him up, saying that 500,000 children under age 5 would be alive today if sanctions did not exist. Surely Iraqi children are not enemies of international peace and security, the waiter expostulated, even if their ruler is a brutal dictator. The United States presses for continued sanctions because Hussein is flouting United Nations resolutions, but stands by Israel when it has flouted UN Resolution 242 (which urges Israel to withdraw from land occupied in the 1967 War) for over 30 years. Arabs and Muslims suffer from these and other US policies.

The only logic this young Egyptian could see was that America was pursuing a worldwide war against Islam, in which the victims were overwhelmingly Muslim. America is a democracy, he concluded, so Americans must hate Muslims to endorse this war.[9]

Toensing suggests to the young Egyptian that while his premises may be correct, his conclusion is false. The United States may be a democracy, but Americans do not have much input on US foreign policy, they do not choose the allies and adversaries of their government. Americans do not vote on the foreign aid agenda, there are no referenda on whether Israel should or should not be supported in all cases or whether the US government should veto this or that UN resolution. Americans have a fundamental sense of fairness, says Toensing, but they rarely have accurate *information* about the effect of their country's foreign polices. So, to what use, the young Egyptian could legitimately have asked, do you put your democracy and freedom?

America's question, then, is not unique. It is mirrored among the 'people' America is trying to understand, define and specify, the crowd from among whom come the terrorists. From the perspective of the young Egyptian waiter and many Muslims, it is America who hates Muslims; and their own hatred of America emerges from this perception.

Toensing admits to the Egyptian waiter and his friends that 'Hollywood stereotypes of Arabs and Muslims as wild-eyed, Koran-waving fanatics' do enforce the perception that Muslims are only there to be hated and despised.[10] He could have added that people the world over get the same impression from much American journalism and scholarship. When the *Toronto Star* sent one of its reporters to wander around local bookshops and see what 'hate literature' he could find, the reporter made a surprising discovery. In one of the stores' magazine sections, he came across

a Dec. 3, 2001 issue of the *National Review*, with a drawing of George Bush as a medieval crusader on the cover, contain[ing] an article headlined 'Martyred: Muslim murder and mayhem against Christians', in which the author cites with approval the conclusion in Samuel Huntington's book, *The Clash Of Civilizations And The Remaking Of World Order*: 'The underlying problem for the West is not Islamic fundamentalism. It is Islam, a different civilization whose people are convinced of the superiority of their culture and are obsessed with the inferiority of their power'. This is certainly a long way from *Mein Kampf*, but a Muslim browser in the store who came across this statement might be forgiven for feeling a distinct chill in the air.[11]

Or as the noted Palestinian writer Edward Said, for many years a resident of New York and teacher at Columbia University, commented in an article for *Al Ahram Weekly*:

I do not know a single Arab or Muslim American who does

not now feel that he or she belongs to the enemy camp, and that being in the United States at this moment provides us with an especially unpleasant experience of alienation and widespread, quite specifically targeted hostility.[12]

When stereotypes are the norm, mirror reflects mirror, like one of those fairground attractions that present more and more distorted images. Take, for example, the article in *National Review* by Contributing Editor Ann Coulter, under the headline 'This is War':

This is no time to be precious about locating the exact individuals directly involved in this particular terrorist attack. Those responsible include anyone anywhere who smiled in response to the annihilation of patriots like Barbara Olsen ...

People who want our country destroyed live here, work for our airlines, and are submitted to the exact same airport shakedown as a lumberman from Idaho. This would be like having the Wehrmacht immigrate to America and work for our airlines during World War II. Except the Wehrmacht was not so bloodthirsty ...

We should invade their countries, kill their leaders and convert them to Christianity. We weren't punctilious about locating and punishing only Hitler and his top officials. We carpet bombed German cities, we killed civilians. That's war. And this is war.[13]

Coulter's rage at being a target of hatred ends up reflecting exactly the offence complained of. It is a defiant refusal to know anything further about the context and circumstances in which other people live, think and are affected by events.

Then there was Rich Lowry at *National Review* online – 'America's premier conservative website' – who reported 'Lots of sentiment for nuking Mecca'. He commented:

This is a tough one, and I don't know quite what to think. Mecca seems extreme, of course, but then again few people would die and it would send a signal. Religions have suffered such catastrophic setbacks before ... And, as a general matter, the time for seriousness – including figuring out what we would do in retaliation, so maybe it can have a slight deterrent effect – is now rather than after thousands and thousands more American casualties.[14]

Lowry and Coulter identify with popular sentiment and articulate opinions common enough on the streets, but is this groundswell of emotion what shapes policy, determines political and military response? Within America, people understand that a spectrum of opinion exists, and how it operates. Populist rabble-rousing has a context, and the polarisation of opinion is now the staple of 24-hour news channels, the gladiatorial arena in which issues are not so much debated as wielded like blunt instruments. Yet America presents itself as a nation newly reconfirmed in unity of purpose. So should other people disregard or take serious notice of Coulter and Lowry? If their rhetoric is background noise, not serious political debate, should we question whether the same distinctions operate elsewhere? Is the background noise of stereotypes and cultural clichés preventing Americans from learning more about the range of opinions among those people they desperately seek to understand?

To find the stereotype is to think we have found the answer, when all we have stumbled across is the nub of the problem. So where do we turn? Our question needs answers grounded in *knowledge*. Where do we look to fill the information gap? As Said argued in his *Al Ahram* article:

[T]he media have run far to many 'experts' and 'commentators' on terrorism, Islam, and the Arabs whose endlessly repetitious and reductive line is so hostile and so misrepresents our history, society and culture that the media itself has become little more than an arm of the war on terrorism in Afghanistan and elsewhere ...[15]

Edward Said is the author of the classic study *Orientalism* (1978), which concerns the tradition in literature and scholarship by which Western civilisation represents and perceives Islam and Muslims. Said is not the only scholar who has demonstrated how scholarly ideas support, inform and sustain popular stereotypes. The basic representation of Muslims as militant, barbaric fanatics, corrupt, effete sensualists, people who lived contrary to natural law, developed early in Western scholarship and has been resistant to change. And its central premise has always been that the failings of Muslims, as people and societies, stem from their beliefs. What medieval Europe made of Islam and Muslims has been described by British historian Norman Daniel as 'knowledgeable ignorance', defining a thing as something it could not possibly be, when the means to know it differently were available.[16] Most importantly, scholarly Orientalism supports the idea that the natural consequence of Muslim beliefs is the characteristics of the standard stereotype. Conformity and orthodoxy are seen as central to the nature of a monolithic Islamic civilisation. It is conventional not to examine the range of opinion that exists in Muslim society, not to see its people and history as shaped by a civilisational discourse, but to see the extreme as the norm.

The authority of Orientalism as knowledge has immense practical consequences. It structures the learned books as well the popular press, it finds its outlets in plasterboard movie villains as well as in strategic political thinking. But most of all, it provides an edge of fear and discomfort in the relations between ordinary people, the non-Muslim and Muslim populations of Europe and America. Racism and discrimination across North America exist not only in the attitudes and actions of an obnoxious extreme fringe – they can be implicit in the commonplace attitudes and information of well-meaning, well-intentioned, nice, sensible people.

But how can knowledge be 'knowledgeable ignorance'? Orientalism is not exactly unique. For centuries, scholars asserted that Africans were an 'inferior' race, natural slaves, 'hewers of wood and drawers of water'. It was not prejudice that created the 'peculiar institution', as slavery in the Southern states of the US was euphemistically known – slavery was supported by science and structured scientific investigation of the anatomy, biology and then the genetic make-up of different races. The legacy of this discredited body of knowledge has not evaporated, as we saw in the controversy surrounding *The Bell Curve* (1994), which argued that there is a natural class of Americans, mainly blacks, who are deficient in intelligence and the cognitive abilities required to deal with the information society.[17] Such ideas are now generally accepted as wrong, not only wrong-headed but a clear misuse of science and knowledge. The political and social consequences of attitudes that depended on this knowledge, however, still bedevil race relations between black and white in America. Unpicking the racism woven into the fabric of American society has been a long, painful process, and is still unfinished business. Muslim Americans, along with Muslims the world over, have another item to add to the agenda of necessary business: surmounting the legacy of history, undoing the political, social and cultural consequences of Orientalism. In times of crisis, it is both harder and more necessary to question what we know and take for knowledge.

Thus, Orientalism makes Muslims incomprehensible yet predictable. The persistence of this perspective, the consistent resort to the same set of perceptions in scholarly works, literature, history and political studies, as well as in Hollywood films, leads to the conclusion that Islam and the West have been engaged in a clash of civilisations since Prophet Muhammad began preaching his Message in 610 AD. Orientalism is another hall of mirrors in which the distorted images are not merely popular stereotypes, but *cultural knowledge*.

In the light of this, is it surprising that many in the West see today's 'war on terrorism' as the prelude to a renewed clash of civilisations? The question is in every newspaper and magazine. It did not need the right-wing American political scientist Samuel Huntington to pose the question – the idea has never actually gone away. There is a sense in which Osama bin Laden is utterly predictable as a demon leading the charge of his civilisation, since he embodies so many of the essential details of the time-honoured image that the West expects from a Muslim iconoclast in ideas, rhetoric and action.

Should we therefore be surprised if American public opinion understands the events of 9-11 as the deadly fulfilment of Orientalist predictions? Yet the reality of the situation is more complex than that. 'Not everyone hates us', says Joseph S. Nye, Dean of the Kennedy School of Government at Harvard, 'nor is bin Laden the only catalyst for terror. The Aum Shinrikyo cult that spread chemical poisons in the Tokyo subway system a few years ago was interested in fomenting a war between the United States and Japan. And Timothy McVeigh [the Oklahoma City bomber] was a homegrown product. The important question is whether such hard nuggets of hatred can broaden their appeal beyond their narrow band. The answer to that depends in part on what the United States represents and what it does.'[18]

What the US represents and does has upset a lot of people – not least the array of left-wing intellectuals whom we encountered in chapter one. But it would be wrong to assume that everyone in the non-Western world has a uniform opinion of America. The Kuwaiti royalty, for example, has a great deal to thank America for – and takes every opportunity to show its love and affection for the US. But while the Kuwaitis thank America for supporting their cause (liberating them from Iraqi occupation), the Palestinians hate America for not supporting their cause and not restraining Israel. In general, the élites of the Third World who have benefited directly from American aid or business deals, and the regimes that are kept in power with American assistance, such as Saudi Arabia and Egypt, have little reason to dislike the US. It is those who see themselves, for whatever reason, as victims of American power and policies who have a real grudge. And these people include not only the billion or so inhabitants of the planet who blame the International Monetary Fund's 'structural adjustment' programmes (and hence America) for going to bed hungry every night; or all those in Asia and Africa who point accusing fingers at American multinational corporations for appropriating their natural resources, from their livestock gene-plasm to well-established traditional medicines; or those who perceive themselves, rightly or wrongly, to be victims of American intervention in Latin America; but also the French, who feel that their culture is under threat by the juggernaut of American-led globalisation; and the Japanese and South Koreans, who feel it is time that they said 'No' to America. Clearly, 'the people' who would have a reason to, or could be perceived to, hate America form a large constituency. We shall explore many of these sources of 'hatred', both Western and non-Western, in following chapters.

And there is one other aspect to this question of hatred. The word itself has so many uses and gradations. 'I hate overcooked eggs.' 'I hate rap music.' 'I hate racial prejudice.' The point is so obvious that it has to be mentioned: it is perfectly possible to profoundly disagree with something, indeed to believe that rap music or racial prejudice or any other 'hateful' item should not exist or be tolerated, to genuinely loathe and detest it, and still be capable of peaceful co-existence in a world in which it exists. The glib way in which genuine political differences are consigned to hatred, and criticisms of American actions and policy become anti-Americanism or 'un-American activities', is a recipe for ending debate, not for making greater sense of mutual differences.

So 'hate' is an ambiguous term. But there is one connotation of hatred that the events of 9-11 made inescapable: evil. The 'people' who hate America are frequently labelled as 'evil' – 'evil men', 'evil doers', 'the axis of evil'. The fact that 9-11 was an evil act, in the dictionary sense of being 'morally bad, wicked and harmful', is beyond doubt. But evil is not only a complex notion, one with which Western philosophers have struggled for centuries; it is also a double-edged sword. The question 'Why do people hate America?' itself turns on the nature of evil.

Pure evil has no solution. It can only be eradicated, and attempts to eradicate evil generate as many problems as they solve, if not more. All religions teach that the history of human existence is the struggle with evil. Describing people in terms of pure evil is seductive because it requires no self-reflection, no assessment of any context and contributory circumstances. The transition to evil as an explanation resolves all of the ambiguities that attach to hatred, and much more. As British journalist Barbara Gunnell noted in the *New Statesman*, it becomes an invitation to 'identify an enemy'. Both the American administration and the Taliban leadership describe each other in the terminology of evil. While President Bush declared that 'our war is war against terrorism and evil', Mullah Mohammad Omar, the leader of the Taliban regime, reacted by saying that he would never accept the government that the US, with UN support, put together in Afghanistan because it was made up of 'evil doers'. Mullah Omar also declared that 'America has created the evil that is attacking it'. Such summary judgements are not very enlightening. 'The "axis of evil" tells us nothing about, for example, the actions of the citizens of Iraq or Iran or North Korea (far less their relations with each other)', writes Gunnell. 'It is merely an invitation to identify our enemies. By talking of them as "evil", we do not need to ask why they act as they do, feel outraged or oppressed, opt for suicidal terror rather than protest or political engagement. The questions to which we all need answers since 11 September fall off the agenda in the face of the description "evil". Evil simply demands opposition rather than analysis or understanding.'[19]

Evil is a moral issue, but a far more complex one than simplistic political rhetoric allows. We are reminded of T.S. Eliot's chilling phrase in *Murder in the Cathedral*, that 'sin grows with doing good'. The essence of moral judgement is self-scrutiny, the willingness to submit to examination what Eliot elsewhere called 'things ill done and done to other's harm / Which once you took for exercise of virtue' (*The Four Quartets*). Even the most powerful do not necessarily have sufficient information or control to appreciate the possible or actual consequences of their decisions. It is a cliché to say that we can all be wise with hindsight, but Eliot's phrase suggests something much more difficult and troubling – the fact that from certain perspectives, our assumptions about good and evil are not moral judgements at all, but self-interested, partial assessments. We have the capacity to do what we take to be good and nevertheless cause evil for ourselves or other people. Only by careful examination and considering things from many different angles can we get any sense of which is which.

The targets of attack on 9-11 were deliberate, and their selection directly related to the question of why people hate America. The World Trade Center, when built the tallest skyscraper in the world, was a symbol of the global economy in a globalising economic order. It had its foundations deep in the soil of the most cosmopolitan city in the richest nation on Earth. The Pentagon is the command centre of the military might of the most powerful nation in human history. America, the single superpower, is now, uniquely, a *hyperpower*. Earthly power, it uses and abuses, how it is experienced by people who are not Americans – these are avenues of investigation that clearly trouble Americans in the aftermath of this tragedy. It is not just governments and statesmen who have to be concerned about the exercise of virtue that may end up doing harm to others, and thus become a vice that enables sin to grow by doing good. As Ronald J. Herring, Director of the Mario Einaudi Center for International Studies at Cornell University, told a gathering for International Education Week: 'American freedom to act on a global stage has left many trampled in our wake. Meaning well – our national self perception – has not been enough. Most Americans have not studied our foreign policy through the lens of its objects – or at all.' Herring specifically disagrees with President Bush's answer that 'they hate our freedoms'. For him, a better answer is that people in many parts of the world resent American abuse of power more than American freedom:

> Those who feel marginalized, betrayed, humiliated, or wounded by our power are not part of our inter-subjective community. We are just beginning to come to terms with their anger, its distribution and root causes.
>
> Seeking causes has ironically been portrayed as unpatriotic. The obverse is true: if we fail to understand causes we will as a nation exacerbate and replicate the threatening conditions that now afflict us. We will leave fear as a legacy for following generations.[20]

Clearly, how America perceives others and how others perceive America is at the heart of the question we are exploring. America affects, directly and indirectly, the lives of every individual, community and nation on the planet. Thus, all the possible and varied answers to the question 'Why do people hate America?' are relevant not just for Americans but for everyone, everywhere. The poet Robert Burns once wrote: 'I would that God the gift would give us / To see ourselves as others see us.' (Or, as the purists would have it in its original 'untranslated' Laland Scots: 'O wad some Pow'r the giftie gie us / To see oursels as others see us!') To see ourselves as we appear in the eyes of other people requires us to forget our own myths and self-perceptions. There are many Americas – including the one that is perceived by the rest of the world, by the victims of American power. Can one America see the other America?

So we come to the final part of the question: America. In an article for *The National Interest* entitled 'Who's Afraid of Mr Big?', the German foreign policy analyst Josef Joffe described America as 'both menace and seducer, both monster and model'.[21]

He is probably right. While Americans want to know why people hate them, the fact is that the entire world has a love-hate relationship with America. The average citizen of any country on earth knows more of America than of any other nation or people. What America thinks of the rest of the world, as projected by its media and dominance of global popular entertainment, is consumed by people everywhere. By contrast, the American public gets less access to foreign news, less exposure to foreign popular culture, and is governed by elected representatives who increasingly have never ventured beyond America.

A vast nation such as America is not a monolith, yet no nation works harder to expound a sense of unity, of common identity, a shared heritage of sustaining ideas and common traditions. No newly independent nation in the Third World is more concerned to inculcate its national ethos in its citizens, or gives more prominence and veneration to its national symbols. What America teaches itself about itself is familiar to the rest of the world through the global reach of its media and consumer culture. And as Joffe suggests, there is a subtle duality in the rest of the world's response to America. The rest of the world is more alert to the contradictions within America and its history than Americans themselves; more intrigued and interested to explore these contradictions than Americans are prepared to participate in such debate. As President Clinton noted in a speech at the University of California in 1997: 'We were born with a declaration of independence which asserted that we all were created equal and a constitution that enshrined slavery. We fought a bloody civil war to abolish slavery but we remained unequal by law for another century. We advanced across the continent in the name of freedom, yet in doing so we pushed Native Americans off their land. We welcome immigrants, but each new wave has felt the sting of discrimination.'[22] Such a comment from a non-American would not be welcome, and would most likely be taken as outright hostility. But in an interconnected world dominated by the reach of American power, the rest of the world cannot avoid taking America and all things American seriously. America can do things otherwise.

But to fully understand the animosity that people feel towards America, we need to recognise how Americans perceive America. And to do this, notes Len Duhl, who teaches at the University of California and has travelled the world as a UNESCO expert on health and urban environments, 'we need to analyse the American unconscious, the place where its myths and self-perceptions are located':

Consider, for example, Big America: big A-Anglo-Saxon, big business. These Americans arrived here from Europe hating their governments. They had been oppressed in Europe. Thus, the perception was always a Horatio Alger myth: 'Do it yourself!' And if you have to do it for others, they must be lesser people who need you. It is a mode of behaviour that is natural and rational to them because it is an integral part of their myth. But, from the perspective of others, it is easy to see that taking that position is demeaning, and it is not unnatural or irrational for others to resent it.

Moreover, America is so big, so self-contained that it is easy for us to forget that the rest of the world does really exist. Or, at least, we don't need it, there is no sense in collaboration. We are in charge. Again, the myth that America is the world leads to actions that we see as natural but the rest of the world legitimately views with suspicion. Unilateral cooperation, that is cooperation only for the sake of political expediency, is pure paternalism – and shows contempt for others. When America ignores such issues as pollution and global warming it sends out the signal that the only thing that matters in the world is America. It is hardly surprising that those who have to live with the consequences of pollution and global warming do not look towards America with love and affection.

Then again, look at the American media. It transmits a

constant and perpetual message of uncontrolled wealth, power, violence, crime and aggressiveness. The pop music does the same. That's a helluva thing to export as our image. And it is an image that comes naturally to America because it is there in our founding myths.[23]

We will take a closer look at the founding myths and narratives of America, and how these myths have shaped America's self-image, in chapters five and six. First, let's see how most of the rest of the world perceives America and what has been the experience of other people, over the last five decades, of American political and cultural power.

CHAPTER THREE

America and the World as America

' Sometimes the truth hurts.' The motto of *Alias*, the ABC television series about a graduate student who moonlights as a top secret agent, has a great deal to teach us all. *Alias* has been described as superb, no apologies, escapist entertainment. But this slick, breathless show with its totally preposterous plot also tells us a great deal about America and how America sees the world.

We suggested in chapter one that films and television simultaneously reflect 'reality' and construct it. As the Italian novelist and critic Umberto Eco has noted, they do not just *transmit* an ideology; they *are* themselves an ideology. *Alias* is American ideology writ large. In the show, the vivacious and athletic Sydney Bristow discovers that her secret service employers, SD-6, are not a secret division of the CIA, but enemies of the free world. She is in fact not fighting for American values, but on behalf of America's adversaries. Sydney seeks the aid of the real CIA and becomes a double agent: her mission is to complete the cases at SD-6 while reporting her findings back to the CIA. But neither Sydney nor we the viewers can tell the difference between the goals and values of SD-6 and those of the real CIA. Soon, Sydney discovers that her estranged father, ostensibly working for SD-6, is not only a double agent for the CIA but also an FBI operative, her mother was a KGB assassin, and intelligence agencies around the world are engaged in a deadly battle to capture a 500-year-old book in which a Renaissance Italian inventor sketched blueprints for 21st-century technology!

Sydney, like America itself, has a dual personality. As her normal self, she is the personification of innocence and virtue, constantly anxious and insecure, trying hard to improve her college grades, comforting her lovelorn room-mate, lamenting the loss of her fiancé, angry about her alienated father, thinking about her mother, and fending off advances from her goofy reporter friend. There is much introspection, drinking and curling up on overstuffed sofas, and sensitive and humane exchanges, in her normal life. But once she is off on a mission, Sydney turns into a fighting machine. Aided by the latest technology (dispensed by a dopey geek in SD-6), she fights like the Terminator, delivering chin-high kicks, jumping from skyscrapers and snapping car antennae into the eyes of her attackers. She is totally cool and totally determined, even when villainous interrogators are yanking out one of her molars with pliers. Every episode ends with Sydney in mortal danger, which she transcends with absolute confidence and unmitigated professionalism.

For *Alias*, America is the world. An average episode may move with lightning speed from Los Angeles to Cairo and Moscow, Rome and Oxford, Tuscany and Geneva, Madrid and São Paulo, from a mental institution in Bucharest to a desert in Argentina, before returning to Los Angeles. The rest of the world is essentially America's veranda, where the villains – enemies of the CIA as well as SD-6 – all recognisable as 'other' people, are firmly put in their place. No matter where Sydney's missions take her, with the exception of minor details and a few quaint natives, everywhere looks just like Los Angeles, where the show is filmed. Wherever she looks, Sydney has the same perspective. Not surprisingly, she moves through the non-American world as though it were her own backyard; and returns from each mission as if she had popped out to the local shopping mall. And her enemies, too, are everywhere and come in all shades of colour: Arabs, Chinese, Russians, Cubans – all acting as independent, covert networks.

What *Alias* shows with great confidence is not that America *wants* to rule the world, but the more natural fact that it *is* ruling the world. Nation states, geographical boundaries, political structures are not important; what is significant is groups of feuding networks chasing their interests on the world stage. There are no competing powers because there is only one power, only one source of law and order. In such a natural order, it makes little sense to talk of Empire and American imperialism; indeed, such rhetoric and analysis are dangerously obsolete. Empires require colonies in which unwilling folks are forced into becoming subject people; imperialism entails a dominating metropolis trying to capture the markets and impose its rule on a distant country. Today, the globe is much more like an extension of American society, where – mostly – all too willing individuals and communities embrace American culture and values. Distance, as *Alias* shows so vividly, has lost its meaning. Apart from odd 'rogue states', there are hardly any 'distant countries' that need to be 'influenced' by naked imperialism. America is thus not so much an old-fashioned imperial power seeking its 'spheres of influence' and competing with other imperial powers: it is a hyperpower with no equivalent. Hardly surprising, then, that *Alias* perceives the world as America. America is the world; and the world is America.

If the world is America, then it follows as a natural corollary that the interests of America should be the interests of the world. And all those who act against the interests, or culture, or world-view, of America are in fact acting against the welfare and security of the world. These states and groups of people are like so many muggers, scoundrels and criminals that one finds in any American ghetto; and they have to be brought to justice wherever they are as speedily and efficiently as possible. This has been the logic of American military interventions for well over a century. Indeed, America has militarily intervened in other countries with as much ease and frequency as Sydney, the super double agent, goes on her overseas missions. The US has sent its troops to places as far off as China, Korea, Vietnam and Indonesia, and as close to home as Costa Rica, Guatemala and Grenada.

As early as 1823, President James Monroe established what became known as the Monroe Doctrine – that the American hemisphere was, henceforth, off limits to European adventurism, any example of which America would view as 'dangerous to our peace and safety'. What happened in the Americas was of direct concern to the United States, and on this premise there is hardly a Latin American country that has not suffered at the hands of America. Most recently in Chile in 1973, the US brought down the democratically elected government of Salvador Allende and installed the right-wing military dictator General Augusto Pinochet. Allende was not some newly-invented iconoclast: he had long been part of the internal political process of Chile. Not only was Allende assassinated, but thousands of left-wing supporters were rounded up, tortured and murdered – American citizens among them – with the connivance and support of the US government.

Then there is Nicaragua, where in the 1980s the US fought a bitter, protracted war against the left-wing Sandinistas. This intervention was an almost exact re-run of 1927, when President Calvin Coolidge authorised the twelfth military incursion in Nicaragua in less than three-quarters of a century to overthrow the Liberal Party, among whose leaders was Augusto César Sandino. Sandino's liberals, like the latter-day Sandinistas named in his honour, were, according to the US, 'impregnated with Bolshevist ideas'. As the hearings on the Iran–Contra scandal established,[1] the United States government maintained its funding and support for the insurgent Contras in defiance of Congressional resolutions and with the proceeds of drug trafficking. The rationale for opposing the Sandinistas and supporting the Contras (who were renowned for their intimidation, murder and torture of innocent Nicaraguans) was that, as 'Bolshevists', the Sandinistas were the antithesis of democracy. And yet, in February 1990 the 'undemocratic' Sandinistas were defeated in national elections in Nicaragua and left office. Furthermore, on three subsequent occasions Daniel Ortega has led the Sandinista party in elections and three times accepted the negative verdict of the Nicaraguan electorate. A majority of Nicaraguans, beyond the immediate issues of their domestic politics, also calculate that their country is safer and more likely to enjoy peace, whatever else it may lack, without Ortega in government to provoke the US into further intervention.

In October 1983, the US launched an invasion against the tiny island of Grenada; and so the list goes on. The United States has repeatedly intervened both militarily and through covert action in almost every Latin American state: Bolivia, Brazil, Colombia, Cuba, Dominica, Ecuador, El Salvador, Guatemala, Haiti, Honduras, Jamaica, Mexico, Panama, Peru, Surinam, Uruguay. Ostensibly, these interventions have been in defence of 'democracy', 'human rights' and 'freedom', but somehow they always end up securing markets for America. They have taken place to support or bring to power some of the most noted violators of 'democracy', 'human rights' and 'freedom'. Those who have paid the price for securing the vital interests of the United States have been ordinary, innocent citizens of these countries who have been slaughtered, imprisoned, tortured and maintained in illiberal economic structures inherited from Spanish colonialism that perpetuate abject poverty and all the ills consequent on lack of equal opportunity.

Immediately after the tragedy of 11 September, Zoltan Grossman, an American peace activist and regular contributor to the radical magazine *Counterpunch*, published a list of 'A Century of US Military Interventions from Wounded Knee to Afghanistan', based on Congressional Records and the Library of Congress Research Service (the list is reproduced at the end of this chapter). Grossman lists 134 interventions, small and big, global and domestic, covering 111 years between 1890 and 2001. Up to the end of World War II, the list shows, the US made an average of 1.15 interventions per year; that increased to 1.29 during the Cold War. After the fall of the Berlin Wall, the interventions increased further to 2.0 per year. So, as US hyper-imperialism expanded, the interventions increased to protect its 'interests'. Moreover, as Johan Galtung, director of Transcend (a Network for Peace and Development) shows in *Searching for Peace* (2002), the spatial patterns of the interventions also changed drastically in the post-war period.[2] The first focus of US intervention was on East Asia (Korea, Vietnam, Indonesia; but also Iran), and was extremely violent. The second was on Eastern Europe (including the Soviet Union), but due to the presence of a counter superpower, the interventions were not overtly violent. The third phase was in Latin America, starting in Cuba and reaching most of the continent. The violence this time was both micro and macro, but did not reach the extent of the violence in East Asia. The fourth phase focused on West Asia, starting with Palestine and Iran, then Libya and Lebanon/Syria, and moved on in the 1990s to Iraq, and at the beginning of the 21st century to Afghanistan. So the interventions move from Confucian-Buddhist societies to Orthodox Christian and Catholic Christian cultures, and finally to Islamic civilisation.

The rest of the world acquires much of its popular perception of America, and of what America thinks of the rest of world, through television series like *Alias* and Hollywood films like *Executive Action* and *The Siege*. But this perception is also based on concrete experience – for example, how the US behaves at international forums such as the United Nations. Indeed, US behaviour at the UN is not far removed from that of SD-6 in *Alias*: since we control the world, we can do very much as we like. As the former UN Secretary-General Boutros

Boutros-Ghali writes in his book *Unvanquished: a US–UN Saga*, the UN is now the sole property of a single power – the US – which, through intimidation, threats and the use of its veto, manipulates the world body for the benefit of its own interest.[3] When it suits the US, it uses the UN to seek legitimacy for its actions, to build coalitions and impose sanctions on 'rogue states'. When world opinion goes against the US, it treats the UN with utter contempt. In the aftermath of World War II, the US was a prime mover in establishing the UN – and such UN initiatives as the Universal Declaration of Human Rights – as an institution to further 'democracy' and 'freedom' on the Western model as a global norm. Throughout the history of the UN, America has consistently vetoed any resolution or declaration that did not reflect US priorities or business interests. 'With note-worthy regularity', writes William Blum in *Rogue State* (2001), 'Washington has found itself – often alone, sometimes joined by one or two other countries – standing in opposition to the General Assembly resolutions aimed at furthering human rights, peace, nuclear disarmament, economic justice, the struggle against South African apartheid and Israeli lawlessness and other progressive causes'. Blum lists some 150 incidences between 1984 and 1987 when the US cast a solitary 'no' vote against General Assembly resolutions.[4]

This despite the fact that the US did not pay its UN dues for decades. When it finally agreed to pay past dues in return for a reduction in its assessments, it refused to fulfil the promise. The resentment against the US at typical UN meetings is so intense that it can be felt in the air. It was this resentment that led the UN's Economic and Social Council (ECOSOC) to oust the US from the 53-member Human Rights Commission (HRC) in May 2001. It was the first time this had happened since the Commission was created in 1946. The ECOSOC voted in a secret ballot, and one would expect such a move to be led by Third World nations with long lists of grievances. In fact, it was the vote of a number of European and 'friendly nations' that eventually ousted America. The US suffered a similar defeat in 1998 when it was ejected from, but later reinstated to, the UN Advisory Committee on Administrative and Budgetary Questions (ACABQ), a key committee that deals with funding in the whole body.

The US has consistently opposed the important human rights initiatives of the United Nations. It is one of only two countries – the other being Iraq – that has still not ratified the 1989 landmark UN Convention on the Rights of the Child. It also held back ratifications on the treaty to ban landmines and the treaty to establish an International Criminal Court. According to the UN Committee against Torture, which oversees and monitors actions of Parties to the Convention, the US has consistently violated the World Convention against Torture: the Green Berets routinely tortured their prisoners in Vietnam during interrogation, the CIA frequently tortured suspected infiltrators of Soviet émigré organisations in Western Europe, the US trained and maintained SAVAK, the notorious secret service of the Shah of Iran, and trained and equipped the intelligence services of Bolivia, Uruguay, Brazil and Israel with techniques and technologies of torture – to give just a few examples. As Blum notes, in 1982 and 1983 the US was alone in voting against a declaration that education, work, healthcare, proper nourishment and national development are human rights. It would appear that even 13 years later, official American attitudes had not 'softened'. In 1996, at a UN-sponsored World Food Summit, the US took issue with an affirmation by the summit of the 'right of everyone to have access to safe and nutritious food'. The United States insisted that it does not recognise a 'right to food'. For the people of developing nations, these rights – set out and championed by the world community as global norms – are part of their defence against tyranny, corruption and injustice practised within their nations and by agencies and corporations from foreign nations. Within the context and history of Third World nations, establishing these principles as rights opens debates about the legacy of injustices that still create inherent inequalities, poverty and lack of equal opportunity; and it offers the prospect of change. Washington, instead, has championed just one cause: free trade.[5]

If America is the world, it does not need the World's institution to run its foreign and economic policies. In general, the US takes little interest in bodies such as the United Nations Development Programme (UNDP), the United Nations Educational, Scientific and Cultural Organisation (Unesco) and the United Nations High Commission for Refugees (UNHCR). One institution in which America maintains total control is the World Trade Organisation (WTO). Indeed, it has been suggested that the WTO is a major instrument for maintaining American 'neo-imperialism'. But this takes us back to an obsolete mode of analysis in its comparisons with European empires. Today, technology is the glue that binds production, distribution and marketing systems, connects producers, designers and consumers, and enables capital and cultural commodities to whiz around the globe without any regard for borders. As we see in *Alias*, it is technology that enables Sydney to perform her mission with such accomplished ease. Wherever she travels in the world, she is constantly in communication with her handlers. She can open a safe deposit box in a high-security bank within seconds using laser cutters, summon CIA helicopters for help in the middle of an Argentinian desert, and copy huge computer hard disks instantly from great distances. Similarly, it is the all-embracing reach and omnipotence of its technology that enables America to function as a hyperpower. In a hyperlinked world, in which $1.5 trillion change hands in a single day, all the aces are held by those who generate both the technology and the information – all of which leads to a new, heightened hyper-imperialism.

The forums of choice for maintaining US hyperpower, and technological hyper-imperialism, include not just the WTO but also the International Monetary Fund (IMF) and the World Bank. There are two main reasons. First, the WTO, IMF and

World Bank are the most untransparent and undemocratic global institutions. The secrecy surrounding their decision-making processes makes them ideal bodies for keeping the rest of the troublesome world firmly at arm's length. Second, both the WTO and IMF have effective mechanisms for the enforcement of obligations, particularly those of the developing countries: the WTO through the threat of retaliation against their export of goods, and the IMF through loan conditions, which are imposed ruthlessly. The US uses these mechanisms to keep the developing countries in line, and to smooth the progress of its own multinational companies by removing obstacles and giving positive encouragement. By American-imposed convention, the top jobs at the WTO, IMF and World Bank are shared by the US and Europe. When the first person from a developing country, Supachai Panitchpakdi of Thailand, emerged as a viable candidate to head the WTO, all hell broke loose. The then US President, Bill Clinton, threatened a permanent grid-lock at the WTO unless America's chosen candidate was accepted. 'In evaluating the candidates', he explained, he had 'focussed on their positions on issues of importance to us'; this consideration, according to Clinton, was synonymous with 'what we believe would best serve the needs of the WTO'.[6] Not surprisingly, 'a United Nations-appointed study team has labelled the World Trade Organisation a "nightmare" for developing countries', said the *Financial Times*. Its activities 'reflect an agenda that serves only to promote dominant corporatist interests that already monopolise the area of international trade'.[7] And according to the *Economist*, the business bible of the establishment, 'the Fund and Bank ... have become a more explicit tool of western, and particularly American, foreign policy'.[8]

What all this means is that the world's economy functions largely for the benefit of the US and the US-led Group of Seven (G7) countries (Russia, the newest member of this group, making it G8, does not count economically). What the functioning of this global economy means for developing nations is the continuation of structural arrangements that operate to keep them disadvantaged. While such structures continue to operate, development, as known and understood, is the problem and not the cure. What conventional development demands creates the vicious spiral of conditions that work against the interests of the poorest. 'Development' seldom amounts to anything more than developing countries importing expensive – and frequently out-of-date – technologies from the US and other industrialised countries; technologies that they can seldom manage or maintain. Often these technologies undermine local techniques and age-old manufacturing capabilities and end up marginalising the poor even more. This is a paradox that has been known, argued, advanced in pleading terms, but still has not had any effect on the policy stance of the US. If the whole world is read according to one single vision and one set of simplistic 'values', then the complicating conditions of each particular country – its history and how its economic fortunes have been shaped into misfortunes – disappear. The misfortunes of the poorest, however, are a direct by-product of the self-interest of the richest. The US accumulates the wealth of the world through eight types of manipulations, which we will look at in turn.

1. The US has been financing domestic growth through the savings of the rest of the world. 'Ever since the abandonment of the gold standard', says Ed Mayo, the Director of the London-based think tank, New Economic Foundation (NEF), 'the US has benefited from being the currency leader. This means that it benefits from the seignorage, i.e. free money, of issuing dollars for use as cash around the world. It benefits from the right to set interest rates in its domestic interests rather than global interests. One catastrophic effect was when, at the start of the monetarist years of Reagan and Thatcher, the US raised interest rates sky high, precipitating the collapse of Mexico financially and the start of the debt crisis, which has hit poorer countries hard. Since then, many countries have been caught in a debt trap. Many states are

trapped in a vicious spiral of either allowing their currency to float, a tough proposition in the face of the power of the dollar, yen and euro, or tie it to the dollar, so-called dollarisation that came horribly unstuck in Argentina. When countries like Argentina end up in debt, they suffer from capital flight ($130 billion, almost equal to her total public debt), as their US educated élites transfer money out of the country and into US banks', says Mayo.[9] The debt trap is the simple economic equation that has also devastated small farmers in the US. They are encouraged to borrow cheap money to invest in 'development', new equipment, seeds and so on, but however much they borrow or improve, they cannot compete with large-scale operators whose size and resources allow them to control production and the market. So the debt burden grows, and countries – like American small farmers – end up paying, or owing, more in interest than they can possibly earn, however hard they work.

2. The US denies democratic control over their own economic destinies to over two thirds of the world's population. Most of the world has no say at the IMF and little power to initiate positive change at the WTO. In particular, policies tied to IMF loans lead the way to foreign ownership and domination of the economy, especially in the manufacturing and financial sectors. For example, after the South-East Asian economic crisis, the IMF imposed on Thailand and South Korea the condition that they must allow higher foreign ownership of their economies – at the insistence of the US. This was strategically the most crucial of the IMF's conditions, an 'extra bonus' outside of its normal macro-economic conditions (such as raising interest rates, reduction in government expenditure, economic growth and current account deficit). As part of the deal with the IMF, Thailand was asked to allow foreign banks to own more equity in the local banking sector. Through such 'loan conditions', American businesses and technology corporations ended up wholly or partly owning banks, financial institutions and key technology sectors in the developing world.

3. The US interprets 'trade liberalisation' to mean one-way, open access for American multinationals and businesses. Trade liberalisation – that is, removal or reduction of barriers to international trade in goods and services – has been going on since the 1980s. Under the WTO's Agreement on Agriculture (AoA) and the World Bank/IMF-imposed structural adjustment programmes (SAPs), developing countries have to make significant changes in their food and agriculture policies, and open up their economies to cheap food imports, while reducing and limiting support for their farmers. While the AoA itself requires WTO members to reduce tariffs on food imports by 24% over a ten-year period, most SAPs require more sweeping liberalisation measures as well as demand-related measures such as privatisation of state-run enterprises, elimination of subsidies and price controls, and abolition of marketing boards. Ostensibly, the WTO and its Agreement were arrived at by consensus and with the participation of developing countries. In fact, the whole agreement was stitched up by the US and the European Union. AoA has been described as 'an act of fraud' (by Oxfam, amongst others) which intensifies rural poverty and destroys smallholder livelihoods. It enables the US, and the EU, to export its goods cheaply to developing countries in which farmers, unable to compete, are put out of business. The cheap imports come from commercial channels and through dumping of food sold below the cost of production to dispose of surpluses. In Ghana, for example, local farmers are unable to get an economic price for their produce such as corn, rice, soybeans, rabbit, sheep and goats, even in village markets. The farmers are forced to pay heavily for inputs – expensive imported fertilisers and pesticides and sometimes even seeds – and usually receive less for their produce. But food prices for the consumers do not fall. Rural people suffer, despite increases in production, and there is significant deterioration in living standards, primarily among the rural poor. As a result, countless farmers are forced to move to already overburdened cities to eke out some sort of living. Thus,

local agriculture is destroyed, domestic food production is shattered, and the food security of the country is seriously compromised. The story repeats itself from one country to another.

4. The US promotes a type of 'economic freedom' that actually destroys the economic freedom of poor people. It has caught the developing countries in a classic pincer movement: on the one hand, it has opened the terrain for its technology-driven businesses to enter freely and capture the markets of the world; and on the other, it has inhibited the efforts of developing countries to boost their own products and exports, and bars them from US markets. This is what is known as the free market economy. It also goes under the guise of neo-liberalism, which implies a return to the 19th-century liberal or 'laissez faire' economics in which the state had a firmly hands-off stance on economic activities. In fact, the state plays a decisive role in promoting its corporations and businesses. Thus, so-called 'free trade', so aggressively promoted by the WTO and IMF, 'amounts to little more than highway robbery, benefiting only the rich, while making the poor more vulnerable to food insecurity', says Andrew Simms, head of the global economy programme at NEF. 'As a consequence of American policies, in a single day under globalisation, poor countries lose nearly $2 billion due to rigged international trade, 30,000 children die from preventable diseases, and $60 million drains from poor to rich countries in debt.'[10]

5. The US systematically undermines the efforts of the least developed countries to combat poverty and feed their populations. It has imposed massive tariffs on key agricultural items such as rice, sugar and coffee; on groundnuts, for example, it has imposed tariffs of over 100%. These trade restrictions cost the poorer countries of the world a staggering $2.5 billion a year in lost foreign exchange earnings. The overall effects are nothing short of disastrous. In Haiti, for example, the liberalisation of the rice market and subsequent surge in subsidised US

imports has not only destroyed local rice production and the livelihoods of countless farmers, but also undermined national food security. In country after country, in such labour-intensive and job-creating areas as textiles, footwear and agriculture, the dumping of American products, often at a price lower than the cost of production, has shattered the livelihood of vulnerable populations and reduced them to abject poverty.

6. The US defrauds the least developed countries, thus increasing their poverty. Consider, for example, how the Africa Growth and Opportunity Act (AGOA), signed into law by President George W. Bush in October 2001, defrauds the countries of Africa. AGOA is supposed to provide African economies with duty- and quota-free access for their products to the American market in exchange for certain concessions to the US and its firms. So what do the African countries actually get? The American government grants access only to those goods that it decides may not negatively affect US producers. Hence, coffee, sugar and other products of economic benefit to African countries are not covered. In particular, AGOA offers duty- and quota-free access for African textiles and clothing to the American market – but, in fact, only products using fabric and yarns produced in America will have easy access to the US market. Textile products made from materials produced in African countries and other areas will be subject to severe constraints. Access in these cases will be granted only on a yearly basis, and cannot exceed a total of 3.5% of all apparel imported into the US in eight years. Moreover, the US government can withdraw even this benefit at any time, if it determines that there is a sudden surge in imports of textile products into the US which will threaten its own domestic industries. The requirement for US raw material to be used in their products not only undermines the African countries' own domestic raw materials industries, but importing US raw materials for textile production in Africa is expensive, given the transport and other costs involved, which

means that African textile products exported to the US end up being uncompetitive. It is not that they cannot compete, but the rules ensure that they will always be unable to compete fairly on the bottom line. And what does the US get in return? The AGOA demands that African countries must, among other things: (1) eliminate barriers to all US trade and investment in Africa, treat American firms as equal to African firms, and protect US intellectual property to international standards; (2) pursue further privatisation and remove government subsidies and price controls; (3) guarantee international labour standards and set a minimum age for child labour; and (4) not engage in any act that undermines US national security and foreign policy interests. Thus, while America gains real, concrete benefits from AGOA, the benefits for Africa are quite illusory. Such 'agreements' are largely responsible for the increase in absolute poverty in Africa over the last two decades.

7. The US has consistently worked to bring down commodity prices in the developing world. 'Anti-inflation is supposed to be one of the key successes of the US economy over the past decade', says Mayo. 'But the major contributor to low inflation has been the consistent decline in prices for commodities, exported by indebted countries, encouraged to get into exports as a way out of debt by WTO and IMF. For many products such as tea, coffee and groundnuts, the aid- and debt-fuelled oversupply is such that increasing exports from Africa leads to lower overall returns. While the WTO- and IMF-backed push for exports has led to structural oversupply, no cartel of export producers exists, except in oil, to balance power between supply and demand. When cartels have emerged, they have been taken out by US interests, as in the aborted banana cartel in the 1970s, when following the model of OPEC, banana-producing countries in Central and Latin America thought they could do the same. Unfortunately bananas are not like oil, you can't leave them in the ground to restrict supply – they go bad – but even

so, the prime reason for the break-up was the activities of US banana companies like Chiquita that sought to undermine the deal any way they could. It is a buyer's market, in which the principal buyer is the US consumer. It is a recipe for deflation, in which US citizens benefit from price stability and the shock waves are felt in the producer countries – that is, the US has structured a global political economy that, come heads or tails, feeds the US economy.'[11] The lifestyle of the richest nation in the history of the world, based as it is on cheap food, is effectively subsidised by the hard work and continuous effort of the poorest.

8. If all this wasn't enough, the US imposes unilateral coercive economic measures, otherwise known as 'sanctions', with regularity. During the past 80 years, such sanctions have been imposed on various countries on 120 occasions, 104 of them since World War II. In 1998 alone, the US had sanctions against 75 countries, accounting for 52% of the world's population.

Beneficiaries of these manipulations of the global economy are American consumers. When Americans survey the world, they see poverty and under-development that refuses to change. They believe, as they are regularly told by politicians and the media, that America is the world's most generous nation. This is one of the most conventional pieces of 'knowledgeable ignorance'. According to OECD, the Organisation for Economic Cooperation and Development, the US gave between $6 and $9 billion in foreign aid in the period between 1995 and 1999. In absolute terms, Japan gives more than the US, between $9 and $15 billion in the same period. But the absolute figures are less significant than the proportion of gross domestic product (GDP, or national wealth) that a country devotes to foreign aid. On that league table, the US ranks twenty-second of the 22 most developed nations. As former President Jimmy Carter commented: 'We are the stingiest nation of all.'[12] Denmark is top of the table, giving 1.01% of GDP, while the US manages just 0.1%. The United Nations has long established the target of 0.7% of GDP for development assistance, although only four countries actually achieve this: Denmark, 1.01%; Norway, 0.91%; the Netherlands, 0.79%; Sweden, 0.7%. Apart from being the least generous nation, the US is highly selective in who receives its aid. Over 50% of its aid budget is spent on middle-income countries in the Middle East, with Israel being the recipient of the largest single share. More importantly, as the official website of the US Agency for International Development (USAID), proclaims: 'The principal beneficiary of America's foreign assistance program has always been the United States.' The website adds that nearly 80% of USAID contracts and grants go 'directly to American firms', and that USAID programmes have helped to create new markets for American goods and 'hundreds of thousands of jobs'.[13] Far from being a burden on American citizens, aid is that arm of US foreign policy which ensures that the poor are paying a 'tax', effectively subsidising the jobs and companies of the wealthiest nation on earth.

If America is the world, then the world's environmental problems should be seen from the perspective of the United States. The controversy surrounding the Kyoto Protocol illustrates this point well. The Protocol, adopted at the third session of the Conference of the Parties to the United Nations Framework Convention on Climate Change (UNFCCC) in Kyoto, Japan, on 11 December 1997, sets specific targets for the reduction of carbon dioxide emissions. Carbon dioxide, emitted by motor vehicles and industries that burn fossil fuels, is blamed for climate change and global warming. The agreement requires industrialised countries to reduce emissions, by 2012, to an average 5.2% of 1990 levels. But targets vary from country to country; the 15 nations of the European Union, for example, have to reduce emissions to 8% over the period 2008 to 2012, compared to 1990 levels. In March 2001, to the dismay of the international community, the US administration announced that it would not implement the Kyoto Protocol on the grounds that it is not the right tool to deal with the challenge of climate change at a global level – thus putting the whole process of the Protocol in jeopardy. In its place, the Bush administration proposed a 'cap and trade' system that would set limits for emissions of three major air pollutants – but not carbon dioxide. Whereas the Kyoto Protocol sets out mandatory reductions, under the Bush plan, permits would be assigned for each ton of pollution. By cutting emissions, firms would save up these permits for use at a later date, or to trade with other businesses. The European Union estimated that the Bush plan would allow the US to actually increase emissions by up to 33%!

World reaction to the US proposal was unanimous. President Bush's statement was 'the announcement of the death of the Kyoto protocol', said Mohammed Al-Sabban, energy advisor to the Kingdom of Saudi Arabia. 'No one has the right to declare Kyoto dead', declared Sweden's Environment Minister, Kjell Larsson. EU Commission President Romano Prodi announced that 'tearing up the agreement and starting again would be a tragic mistake'. 'I appreciate your point of view', President Bush replied, 'but this is the American position because it's right for America'. And, just to make the point clear, he added: 'We will not do anything that harms our economy, because first things first are the people who live in America.'[14] In a letter to some Republican senators who had urged him to abandon the Kyoto pledge, President Bush gave the reasons for his decision. A new energy department review had concluded that carbon dioxide regulation would lead to significantly higher electricity prices; and he did not want to take action that would harm American consumers during a period of electricity shortages. So the price of electricity in California is far more important than the depletion of the ozone layer, the disappearance of the polar ice caps, the rise in global temperature and the havoc caused throughout the world by climate changes. Not only are the needs of Americans far greater than those of the rest of the world, but even the dangers to the planet as a whole must be subordinated to the desires of American consumers.

If America is the world, then the resources of the world belong to America. This assumption amounts to much more than is suggested by the bare statistics that we come across routinely in the UNDP's Human Development Reports: that Americans consume over half of all the goods and services of the world; that its people spend over $10 billion annually on pet food alone – $4 billion more than the estimated total needed to provide basic health and nutrition for everyone in the world; that their expenditure on cosmetics – $8 billion – is $2 billion more than the annual total needed to provide basic education worldwide; or that the three richest Americans have assets that exceed the combined gross domestic product of the 48 least developed countries. Having cornered most of the world's resources, America now has its eyes firmly set on the last remaining resource of developing countries: the flora, fauna, biodiversity and the very DNA of the indigenous people of the world.

American biotechnology corporations, researchers and speculators are engaged in a quest to appropriate the ancient knowledge and wisdom of indigenous people. The technologies, processes and knowledge of these peoples have developed over thousands of years. They have been domesticating and cross-pollinating plants, taming wild animals, developing plant and herbal medicines, and using techniques that we nowadays associate with biotechnology – employing living organisms, or parts of organisms, to make or modify products, and improve breeds of plant and animal – for centuries. For example, the Igorot people in the Cordillera region of the Philippines have been fermenting their own tapey (rice wine), which is made with a native yeast called bubod, and basi (sugar cane wine), prepared with forest seeds called gamu, for millennia. They have been cultivating and breeding a wide variety of camote (sweet potatoes), which were a staple for them before rice was introduced. And they have developed numerous varieties of rice for different environmental conditions and terrains – a single village may have up to ten varieties of rice seeds planted for different weather and soil conditions. They have similarly developed other varieties of crops such as cassava and taro. While knowledge produced in the US and Europe is aggressively protected, this traditional knowledge has no protection. The WTO's Agreement on Trade-Related Intellectual Property (TRIPs) does not include specific provisions related to the protection of systems, practices, naturally-occurring plants or products that are the basis of traditional and indigenous knowledge. So, American multinational companies, agribusiness and biotechnology firms can appropriate this knowledge and learning with impunity.

Plants that have traditionally been used by indigenous peoples are now the subject of predatory intellectual property claims. It began with the neem plant, which is used in India for making a wide range of medicines for diseases such as ulcers, diabetes, skin disorders and constipation, as well as a potent insecticide effective against locusts, brown plant-hoppers, nematodes, mosquito larvae and beetles. In 1985, a pesticidal neem extract called Margosan-O was patented by a US timber merchant and then sold to M.R. Grace and Co., the multinational chemical corporation. The floodgates were open. Between 1985 and 1995, over 37 patents were granted in Europe and the US to use and develop neem products, including a neem-based toothpaste! So, something that was free and widely available (there are an estimated 14 million neem trees in India alone), something that had been developed and used for centuries by South Asians, became the property of an American multinational corporation. Neem plant was quickly followed by ayahuasca and quinoa from Latin America, kava from the Pacific, and the bitter gourd from the Philippines and Thailand – all widely used by indigenous peoples, but now their ownership is claimed by American business.

This predatory behaviour not only deprives people of what is rightly theirs, but could also have devastating consequences for their future. Consider, for example, what could happen with quinoa (Chenopodium quinoa), a high-protein cereal which has long been a staple in the diet of millions of people in the Andean countries of Latin America. It has been cultivated and developed since pre-Incan times. Two researchers from the University of Colorado received US patent number 5,304,718 in 1994 which gives them exclusive monopoly control over the male sterile plants of the traditional Bolivian Apelawa quinoa variety. So, suddenly, the Andean people cannot use a plant that is a part of their natural ecosystem. Bolivia currently exports this variety to the US and Europe, a market worth US$1 million per year. But if this hybrid variety is used for large-scale commercial production in the US, the Bolivian exports will be prevented from entering US and European markets. This will lead to the displacement of thousands of small farmers, most of whom are indigenous Indians. The other possibility is that lands will fall into the monopoly control of corporations who own the patents (or their subsidiaries in Bolivia), who will produce quinoa using the hybrid commercial varieties. Genetic erosion of the diverse quinoa varieties developed by local farmers over centuries will take place, diminishing forever the genetic diversity. Many farming communities are facing a similar plight throughout the world.[15]

But US bio-piracy is not limited to medicinal plants and crop varieties – it also extends to the DNA of indigenous people. The patent application of the US Department of Commerce for the T-cell line infected with human T-cell lymphotrophic viruses (HTLV) type 1 – which can help in the development of a cure for cancer – of a 26-year-old Guaymi woman from Panama was the first attempt to patent genetic materials from indigenous peoples. This application was submitted as early as 1993. The application was eventually withdrawn after an international outcry and campaigns led by various non-governmental organisations. This, however, did not stop the US National Institute of Health from patenting the DNA of a man from the Hagahai people of the highlands of Papua New Guinea. The patent covered a cell line containing an unmodified Hagahai DNA – and it too had to be withdrawn after international pressure. Since then, attempts to patent the DNA of indigenous people have multiplied – and one can now openly buy Amazonian Indian blood cells on the Internet from US companies.

Indigenous knowledge is, of course, not new knowledge. Genetic engineering is a new science that generates new technology. But the US denies that genetic technology is a new departure from conventional biotechnology, or that it brings with it new environmental and health problems. While it is happy to appropriate ancient knowledge, the US does not want the new technology to be regulated in any way. It has consistently opposed the Convention on Biological Diversity, the first international effort to set legal standards and norms for Genetically Modified Organisms (GMOs) and products derived from or containing GMOs. First, at US insistence, the term 'GMOs' was changed to 'living modified organisms' in the draft Protocol. Second, as scientific evidence mounted on the environmental and health hazards of GMOs and GMO-related products, the US opposed the rest of the world on the question of making the 'Precautionary Principle' the basis for the Protocol. Underlying the use of this principle, which was first formulated in the 1992 Climate Change Convention, is the assumption that biotechnology can generate potentially dangerous outcomes, and that we should proceed with caution and precaution. The principle, now enshrined in many international regulatory statutes, has become the guiding spirit of the European Union's science policy, and is increasingly used in policy-making where there is a perceived risk to the environment or to the health of humans, animals or plants. The US – the biggest developer and exporter of GMOs – is the sole country that rejects the Precautionary Principle. Those developing countries working for a strong bio-safety agreement and promoting the Convention on Biological Diversity are routinely accused by the US of blocking international trade, and it threatens them regularly using the WTO.

Almost every concern of the world, from the risks and safety of GMOs to climate change and biodiversity, from the protection of indigenous knowledge and resources to the reform of undemocratic and authoritarian global institutions like the WTO and IMF, to global justice and fair trade, is reduced by the US to a question of 'free trade' – meaning America should be free to do as it desires. Over the last few decades, that so-called 'free trade' has increased exponentially. Today, one day's trade equals a whole year's commerce in 1949. But while international trade is growing, the regulations designed to manage trade and promote equity are being progressively removed at US behest. In its treatment of the rest of the world, the US acts like an overgrown teenage bully, constantly expressing indignation at having to accept limits on its behaviour while refusing to understand why this behaviour might have real consequences on the lives of others. If it doesn't like a country's economic policies, it crushes them using the WTO and IMF. And if that doesn't work, it imposes sanctions or simply arranges to overthrow its leaders in a coup (Iran, Chile, Guatemala). Authoritarian countries whose leaders are tyrants and brutes who trample on human rights are called friends and allies if they have the right economic policies (Saudi Arabia, the Philippines, El Salvador). The problem is that America's behaviour, its insistence to be free to do as it chooses, is not only placing serious constraints on the freedom of others to choose their own way of life – it is actually placing their very survival in jeopardy. It should not surprise anyone that America is perceived as having declared a war on the non-European world, including the poorest, the weakest, and the most disadvantaged.

But this is a perception of America that Americans seldom have to come to terms with. If America is the world, then what happens in America is of world importance – that is the only thing that Americans need to be aware of. This is why America is comfortable with holding 'World Series' and 'World Championships' in which only Americans participate, as is the case with American football and baseball. From the perspective of the world, the 1996 Olympic Games in Atlanta and the 2002 Winter Olympics in Salt Lake City were held solely for the benefit of America. The rest of the world need not have participated. Just as, in *Alias*, Sydney travels all over the world but does not actually see other societies, other cultures, other environments, or indeed other people (except as villains), or hear other voices, other concerns, so America seldom sees or hears the rest of the world (except as aggressors). As Jim Dator, Professor of Political Science at the University of Hawaii and well known futurist, notes: 'The exclusion of the rest of the world from the American sight is one of the most disturbing facts about American society. Even with its gigantic media system operating with state-of-the-art technologies, the US functions as a society closed to information, facts and opinions of the rest of the world. No wonder Americans as a whole are so unaware of the growing hatred felt for the US in the rest of the world.'[16]

The American media is notoriously parochial. With the exception of a couple of national newspapers, foreign news is, by and large, conspicuous by its absence. Television, the medium that citizens watch and use more than any other, ventures outside the national boundaries only to report disasters and American-led wars. As the American media has acquired a global reach, it has simultaneously, and paradoxically, become even more parochial and banal. Diverse and dissenting voices have been filtered out to create a bland media monoculture dedicated to promoting consumerism, business and the interests of the government and the power élite, and to keeping the masses entertained and docile. This is not the outcome of a 'free market' operating as a natural law – it is the product of conscious state policy.

Since the days of the Reagan administration, the United States has been deregulating its own media industry, and leading an onslaught on international regulation, with the natural consequence that global media power is aggregating into fewer and fewer hands. In 1983, when Ben Bagdikian published *The*

Media Monopoly, media ownership was concentrated in the hands of 50 trans-national conglomerates.[17] In 2002, only nine trans-national firms dominate US and global media: AOL Time Warner, Disney, Bertelsmann, Viacom, News Corporation, TCI, General Electric (owner of NBC), Sony (owner of Columbia and TriStar Pictures and major recording interests), and Seagram (owner of Universal film and music interests). So one global super-industry now provides virtually everything that Americans see and hear on the screen, over the airwaves, in print and on the Web.

These media giants function as a powerful political lobby at the national, regional and global levels. In Washington alone, they spend an estimated $125 million per year lobbying against ownership restrictions. They not only have a heavy hand in drafting national laws and regulations, but also play an important part in shaping and directing international rules and regulations. In 2000, for example, the corporate media giants led the lobbying effort to open up trade with China, and fought against those who raised concerns about free speech and a free press. Earlier, they used US levers to open up Indian markets to satellite television.

Much of what this media cartel purveys to America, Mark Crispin Miller notes in *The Nation*, 'is propaganda, commercial or political'. Under AOL Time Warner, General Electric, Viacom and others, the 'news is, with a few exceptions, yet another version of the entertainment that the cartel also vends nonstop'. These entities, writes Miller,

> are ultimately hostile to the welfare of the people. Whereas we need to know the truth about such corporations, they often have an interest in suppressing it (as do their advertisers). And while it takes much time and money to find out the truth, the parent companies prefer to cut the necessary costs of journalism, much preferring the sort of lurid fare that can drive endless hours of agitated jabbering. (Prior to 9/11, it

was Monica, then *Survivor* and Chandra Levy, whereas, since the fatal day, we have had mostly anthrax, plus much heroic footage from the Pentagon.) The cartel's favored audience, moreover, is that stratum of the population most desirable to advertisers – which has meant the media's complete abandonment of working people and the poor. And while the press must help protect us against those who would abuse the powers of government, the oligopoly is far too cozy with the White House and the Pentagon, whose faults, and crimes, it is unwilling to expose. The media's big bosses want big favours from the state, while the reporters are afraid to risk annoying their best sources. Because of such politeness (and, of course, the current panic in the air), the US coverage of this government is just a bit more edifying than the local newscasts in Riyadh.

Media devoted to the public interest would investigate the poor performance by the CIA, the FBI, the FAA and the CDC, so that those agencies might be improved for our protection – but the news teams (just like Congress) haven't bothered to look into it. So, too, in the public interest, should the media report on *all* the current threats to our security – including those far-rightists targeting abortion clinics and, apparently, conducting bioterrorism; but the telejournalists are unconcerned ... So should the media highlight, not play down, this government's attack on civil liberties – the mass detentions, secret evidence, increased surveillance, suspension of attorney-client privilege, the encouragements to spy, the warnings not to disagree, the censored images, sequestered public papers, unexpected visits from the Secret Service and so on. And so should the media not parrot what the Pentagon says about the current war, because such prettified accounts make us complacent and preserve us in our fatal ignorance of what people really think of us – and why – beyond our borders. And there's much more – about the stunning exploitation of the tragedy, especially by the Republicans; about the links between the Bush and the bin Laden families; about the ongoing shenanigans in Florida – that the media would let the people know, if they were not ... indifferent to the public interest.

In short, the news divisions of the media cartel appear to work *against* the public interest – and *for* their parent companies, their advertisers and the Bush Administration. The situation is completely un-American. It is the purpose of the press to help us run the state, and not the other way around. As citizens of a democracy, we have the right and obligation to be well aware of what is happening, both in 'the homeland' and the wider world. Without such knowledge we cannot be both secure and free.[18]

Such a highly concentrated and controlled media system can hardly be described as a 'free press'. A free press, as the highly regarded author and war correspondent Phillip Knightley noted in *Index on Censorship*, would not reduce the post-11 September debate 'to abuse, incitement, personal attacks, inflammatory accusation and intimidation until many a commentator and intellectual, the very people whose voices we want to hear, have been cowed into silence'.[19] Nor would a free press, as Robert W. McChesney pointed out, uncritically reproduce or broadcast the Pentagon's handouts or work for those who 'benefit by existing inequality and the preservation of the status quo'.[20] The American media functions primarily to keep its American audience ignorant of the rest of the world; it is interested in producing happy consumers, not informed, free-thinking citizens who question the foreign policy of their government. It performs this function largely through self-censorship and subtle bias. Hyper-commercialism has implicit bias against political action, civic values and anti-market activities, and tends to regard consumerism, class inequality and so-called 'individualism' as natural and benevolent. The genius of the American media, as McChesney notes, it its 'general lack of overt censorship. As George Orwell noted in his unpublished introduction to *Animal Farm*, censorship in free societies is infinitely more sophisticated and thorough than in dictatorships, because "unpopular ideas can be silenced, and inconvenient facts kept dark, without any need for an official ban".'[21]

Alias refuses to take itself seriously. It uses all the clichés in the spy genre but does not simply rehash them: it subverts them, pokes fun at the conventions, and laughs at the absurdities of its plot. This is its redeeming feature. America, in contrast, takes itself too seriously. Most Americans take it as a self-evident truth that America has a 'free press', that the US is promoting freedom and human rights across the globe, that the rest of the world is jealous of America's freedom and democracy, that American wealth is a consequence of 'free trade', that the American way of life is the best ever devised in the history of humanity and so America should be loved and admired by everyone; that America, in Lincoln's famous phrase, is 'the last best hope for mankind'. It comes as a great shock to discover that the rest of the world thinks otherwise; that America is an object of much fear and loathing, and that this opinion is based on concrete experience with American power over the last five decades. 'Sometimes the truth hurts.' But as Sydney discovers, unfortunately there is no escaping the truth.

Zoltan Grossman's 'A Century of US Military Interventions from Wounded Knee to Afghanistan'

SOUTH DAKOTA, 1890(–?)
Troops: 300 Lakota Indians massacred at Wounded Knee.

ARGENTINA,1890
Troops: Buenos Aires interests protected.

CHILE, 1891
Troops: Marines clash with nationalist rebels.

HAITI, 1891
Troops: Black workers' revolt on US-claimed Navassa Island defeated.

IDAHO, 1892
Troops: Army suppresses silver miners' strike.

HAWAII, 1893(–?)
Naval, troops: Independent kingdom overthrown, annexed.

CHICAGO, 1894
Troops: Breaking of rail strike, 34 killed.

NICARAGUA, 1894
Troops: Month-long occupation of Bluefields.

CHINA, 1894–5
Naval, troops: Marines land in Sino-Japanese War.

KOREA, 1894–6
Troops: Marines kept in Seoul during war.

PANAMA, 1895
Troops, naval: Marines land in Colombian province.

NICARAGUA, 1896
Troops: Marines land in port of Corinto.

CHINA, 1898–1900
Troops: Boxer Rebellion fought by foreign armies.

PHILIPPINES, 1898–1910(–?)
Naval, troops: Seized from Spain, killed 600,000 Filipinos.

CUBA, 1898–1902(–?)
Naval, troops: Seized from Spain, still hold Navy base.

PUERTO RICO, 1898(–?)
Naval, troops: Seized from Spain, occupation continues.

GUAM, 1898(–?)
Naval, troops: Seized from Spain, still used as base.

MINNESOTA, 1898(–?)
Troops: Army battles Chippewa at Leech Lake.

NICARAGUA, 1898
Troops: Marines land at port of San Juan del Sur.

SAMOA, 1899(–?)
Troops: Battle over succession to throne.

NICARAGUA, 1899
Troops: Marines land at port of Bluefields.

IDAHO, 1899–1901
Troops: Army occupies Coeur d'Alene mining region.

OKLAHOMA, 1901
Troops: Army battles Creek Indian revolt.

PANAMA, 1901–14
Naval, troops: Broke off from Colombia 1903, annexed Canal Zone 1914–99.

HONDURAS, 1903
Troops: Marines intervene in revolution.

DOMINICAN REPUBLIC, 1903–04
Troops: US interests protected in Revolution.

KOREA, 1904–05
Troops: Marines land in Russo-Japanese War.

CUBA, 1906–09
Troops: Marines land in democratic election.

NICARAGUA, 1907
Troops: 'Dollar Diplomacy' protectorate set up.

HONDURAS, 1907
Troops: Marines land during war with Nicaragua.

PANAMA, 1908
Troops: Marines intervene in election contest.

NICARAGUA, 1910
Troops: Marines land in Bluefields and Corinto.

HONDURAS, 1911
Troops: US interests protected in civil war.

CHINA, 1911–41
Naval, troops: Continuous occupation with flare-ups.

CUBA, 1912
Troops: US interests protected in Havana.

PANAMA, 1912
Troops: Marines land during heated election.

HONDURAS, 1912
Troops: Marines protect US economic interests.

NICARAGUA, 1912–33
Troops, bombing: 20-year occupation, fought guerrillas.

MEXICO, 1913
Naval: Americans evacuated during revolution.

DOMINICAN REPUBLIC, 1914
Naval: Fight with rebels over Santo Domingo.

COLORADO, 1914
Troops: Breaking of miners' strike by Army.

MEXICO, 1914–18
Naval, troops: Series of interventions against nationalists.

HAITI, 1914–34
Troops, bombing: 19-year occupation after revolts.

DOMINICAN REPUBLIC, 1916–24
Troops: 8-year Marine occupation.

CUBA, 1917–33
Troops: Military occupation, economic protectorate.

WORLD WAR I, 1917–18
Naval, troops: Ships sunk, fought Germany.

RUSSIA, 1918–22
Naval, troops: Five landings to fight Bolsheviks.

PANAMA, 1918–20
Troops: 'Police duty' during unrest after elections.

YUGOSLAVIA, 1919
Troops: Marines intervene for Italy against Serbs in Dalmatia.

HONDURAS, 1919
Troops: Marines land during election campaign.

GUATEMALA, 1920
Troops: 2-week intervention against unionists.

WEST VIRGINIA, 1920–1
Troops, bombing: Army intervenes against mineworkers.

TURKEY, 1922
Troops: Fought nationalists in Smyrna (Izmir).

CHINA, 1922–7
Naval, troops: Deployment during nationalist revolt.

HONDURAS, 1924–5
Troops: Landed twice during election strife.

PANAMA, 1925
Troops: Marines suppress general strike.

CHINA, 1927–34
Troops: Marines stationed throughout the country.

EL SALVADOR, 1932
Naval: Warships sent during Faribundo Marti revolt.

WASHINGTON DC, 1932
Troops: Army stops WWI vet bonus protest.

WORLD WAR II, 1941–5
Naval, troops, bombing, nuclear: Fought Axis for 3 years; first nuclear war.

DETROIT, 1943
Troops: Army puts down Black rebellion.

IRAN, 1946
Nuclear threat: Soviet troops told to leave north (Iranian Azerbaijan).

YUGOSLAVIA, 1946
Naval: Response to shooting-down of US plane.

URUGUAY, 1947
Nuclear threat: Bombers deployed as show of strength.

GREECE, 1947–9
Command operation: US directs extreme right in civil war.

CHINA, 1948–9
Troops: Marines evacuate Americans before Communist victory.

GERMANY, 1948
Nuclear threat: Atomic-capable bombers guard Berlin Airlift.

PHILIPPINES, 1948–54
Command operation: CIA directs war against Huk Rebellion.

PUERTO RICO, 1950
Command operation: Independence rebellion crushed in Ponce.

KOREA, 1950–3
Troops, naval, bombing, nuclear threats: US and South Korea fight China and North Korea to stalemate; A-bomb threat in 1950, and vs. China in 1953. Still have bases.

IRAN, 1953
Command operation: CIA overthrows democracy, installs Shah.

VIETNAM, 1954
Nuclear threat: Bombs offered to French to use against siege.

GUATEMALA, 1954
Command operation, bombing, nuclear threat: CIA directs exile invasion after new government nationalises US company lands; bombers based in Nicaragua.

EGYPT, 1956
Nuclear threat, troops: Soviets told to keep out of Suez crisis;
Marines evacuate foreigners.

LEBANON, 1958
Troops, naval: Marine occupation against rebels.

IRAQ, 1958
Nuclear threat: Iraq warned against invading Kuwait.

CHINA, 1958
Nuclear threat: China told not to move on Taiwan isles.

PANAMA, 1958
Troops: Flag protests erupt into confrontation.

VIETNAM, 1960–75
Troops, naval, bombing, nuclear threats: Fought South Vietnam
revolt and North Vietnam; 1–2 million killed in longest US war;
atomic bomb threats in 1968 and 1969.

CUBA, 1961
Command operation: CIA-directed exile invasion fails.

GERMANY, 1961
Nuclear threat: Alert during Berlin Wall crisis.

CUBA, 1962
Nuclear threat: Naval blockade during missile crisis; near-war
with USSR.

LAOS, 1962
Command operation: Military build-up during guerrilla war.

PANAMA, 1964
Troops: Panamanians shot for urging canal's return.

INDONESIA, 1965
Command operation: Million killed in CIA-assisted army coup.

DOMINICAN REPUBLIC, 1965–6
Troops, bombing: Marines land during election campaign.

GUATEMALA, 1966–7
Command operation: Green Berets intervene against rebels.

DETROIT, 1967
Troops: Army battles Blacks, 43 killed.

UNITED STATES, 1968
Troops: After King is shot; over 21,000 soldiers in cities.

CAMBODIA, 1969–75
Bombing, troops, naval: Up to 2 million killed in decade of bombing, starvation and political chaos.

OMAN, 1970
Command operation: US directs Iranian marine invasion.

LAOS, 1971–3
Command operation, bombing: US directs South Vietnamese invasion; 'carpet-bombs' countryside.

SOUTH DAKOTA, 1973
Command operation: Army directs Wounded Knee siege of Lakotas.

MIDDLE EAST, 1973
Nuclear threat: World-wide alert during Middle East War.

CHILE, 1973
Command operation: CIA-backed coup ousts elected Marxist president.

CAMBODIA, 1975
Troops, bombing, gas: Captured ship, 28 die in helicopter crash.

ANGOLA, 1976–92
Command operation: CIA assists South African-backed rebels.

IRAN, 1980
Troops, nuclear threat, aborted bombing: Raid to rescue Embassy hostages; 8 troops die in helicopter–plane crash. Soviets warned not to get involved in revolution.

LIBYA, 1981
Naval jets: Two Libyan jets shot down in manoeuvres.

EL SALVADOR, 1981–92
Command operation, troops: Advisors, overflights aid anti-rebel war, soldiers briefly involved in hostage clash.

NICARAGUA, 1981–90
Command operation, naval: CIA directs exile (Contra)
invasions, plants harbour mines against revolution.

LEBANON, 1982–4
Naval, bombing, troops: Marines expel PLO and back
Phalangists, Navy bombs and shells Muslim and Syrian
positions.

HONDURAS, 1983–9
Troops: Manoeuvres help build bases near borders.

GRENADA, 1983–4
Troops, bombing: Invasion four years after revolution.

IRAN, 1984
Jets: Two Iranian jets shot down over Persian Gulf.

LIBYA, 1986
Bombing, naval: Air strikes to topple nationalist government.

BOLIVIA, 1986
Troops: Army assists raids on cocaine region.

IRAN, 1987–8
Naval, bombing: US intervenes on side of Iraq in war.

LIBYA, 1989
Naval jets: Two Libyan jets shot down.

VIRGIN ISLANDS, 1989
Troops: St Croix Black unrest after storm.

PHILIPPINES, 1989
Jets: Air cover provided for government against coup.

PANAMA, 1989–90
Troops, bombing: Nationalist government ousted by 27,000
soldiers, leaders arrested, 2000+ killed.

LIBERIA, 1990
Troops: Foreigners evacuated during civil war.

SAUDI ARABIA, 1990–1
Troops, jets: Iraq countered after invading Kuwait; 540,000
troops also stationed in Oman, Qatar, Bahrain, UAE, Israel.

IRAQ, 1990(–?)
Bombing, troops, naval: Blockade of Iraqi and Jordanian ports, air strikes; 200,000+ killed in invasion of Iraq and Kuwait; no-fly zone over Kurdish north, Shiite south, large-scale destruction of Iraqi military.

KUWAIT, 1991
Naval, bombing, troops: Kuwait royal family returned to throne.

LOS ANGELES, 1992
Troops: Army, Marines deployed against anti-police uprising.

SOMALIA, 1992–4
Troops, naval, bombing: US-led United Nations occupation during civil war; raids against one Mogadishu faction.

YUGOSLAVIA, 1992–4
Naval: Nato blockade of Serbia and Montenegro.

BOSNIA, 1993–5
Jets, bombing: No-fly zone patrolled in civil war; downed jets, bombed Serbs.

HAITI, 1994–6
Troops, naval: Blockade against military government; troops restore President Aristide to office three years after coup.

CROATIA, 1995
Bombing: Krajina Serb airfields attacked before Croatian offensive.

ZAIRE (CONGO), 1996–7
Troops: Marines at Rwandan Hutu refugee camps, in area where Congo revolution begins.

LIBERIA, 1997
Troops: Soldiers under fire during evacuation of foreigners.

ALBANIA, 1997
Troops: Soldiers under fire during evacuation of foreigners.

SUDAN, 1998
Missiles: Attack on pharmaceutical plant alleged to be 'terrorist' nerve gas plant.

AFGHANISTAN, 1998
Missiles: Attack on former CIA training camps used by Islamic fundamentalist groups alleged to have attacked embassies.

IRAQ, 1998(–?)
Bombing, missiles: Four days of intensive air strikes after weapons inspectors allege Iraqi obstructions.

YUGOSLAVIA, 1999(–?)
Bombing, missiles: Heavy NATO air strikes after Serbia declines to withdraw from Kosovo.

YEMEN, 2000
Naval: Suicide bomb attack on USS *Cole*.

MACEDONIA, 2001
Troops: NATO troops shift and partially disarm Albanian rebels.

UNITED STATES, 2001
Jets, naval: Response to hijacking attacks.

AFGHANISTAN, 2001
Massive US mobilisation to attack Taliban, bin Laden. War could expand to Iraq, Sudan, and beyond.

Source: http://www.zmag.org/CrisesCurEvts/Interventions.htm

Publisher's Note: This book went to press before the invasion in Iraq in 2003.

CHAPTER FOUR

American Hamburgers and Other Viruses

There is hardly a place in the world where one cannot get a hamburger. Even in the remote jungles of Sarawak, the rainforests of Brazil, the deserts of North Africa, one cannot escape the 'golden arches' of McDonald's, the 'flaming grills' of Burger King, the cute little girl of Wendy's and other signs and symbols of American food chains. But hamburgers are more than ubiquitous. While the mass-produced hamburger is promoted as food, it is essentially junk, food compounded by a whole series of additives that make the final product of little nutritive value. Moreover, while a hamburger is certainly fast food, it is not, as is commonly claimed, the only or indeed the first fast food the world has ever seen. Every culture has its fast food. The shawarma (a form of rolled-up sandwich) in the Middle East, aloo-puri chaat in India and nasi lamak (rice with dry fish) in South-East Asia, good old British fish and chips and the French baguette with cheese and ham are good examples. So, both as food and as a cultural product, the hamburger pretends to be something it is clearly not.

The hamburger is a particular source of hatred of America. It is the single most concentrated, or should that be congealed, symbol of the entire complex that is America. Like the hamburger, the idea of America has a number of separate ingredients: there is the government, the most powerful government on earth, or the sole hyperpower as we have termed it; there is the history of policy operated by successive American administrations and the consequences of these policies for countries and people beyond America; there is the enormous power of US corporations that can influence the policy of American government to favour their vested interests while remaining beyond the reach of any government to control or make them accountable; then there are the concepts, philosophy and ethos characteristic of the American world-view – such things as individualism and belief in personal freedom – that are like the relishes that flavour the hamburger; and there are Americans themselves, with their particular blend of self-belief, seeming lack of interest in the rest of the world, and certainty that their way of life is the biggest, boldest and best for everyone. Like the hamburger, this multi-dimensional America is reduced and experienced as a standardised, mass-produced, packaged brand. Each aspect of America may have its own distinctive character, and many, taken in isolation, have more good attributes than questionable or negative connotations. But, like the burger, the essence of America is that the individual aspects of its influence seldom occur in isolation. A true hamburger is a superabundant, multi-layered compound entity. It is the degree to which America proclaims and glories in itself as a compound whole that makes the hamburger such a powerful metaphor for the nation, and such a potent symbol and focus for criticism of America in the rest of the world. The hamburger is more than its ingredients – it is, indeed, a way of life.

As a way of life, the hamburger is a seductive novelty with discernible, and deleterious, consequences. Not just because it is an omnipresent con-trick, but also because the consumerism it embodies is seen as a clear cultural threat. It personifies the way in which America is taking over the lives of ordinary people in the rest of the world and shrinking their cultural space – their space to be themselves, to be different, to be other than

America. And America projects itself on the rest of the world as though it were a hamburger: a commodity, a brand, out to capture all cultural space for itself. It sees any negative aspects of its international image not as something rooted in its foreign policy or cultural hegemony, but simply as a communication problem. After 9-11, the Bush administration appointed Charlotte Beers as Under-secretary for Public Diplomacy. Beers, who capped her career by heading two of the world's advertising behemoths, Ogilvy & Mather and J. Walter Thompson, became famous for 'branding' products like American Express. 'Well, guess what?', Secretary of State Colin Powell told senators on the Foreign Relations Committee. 'She got me to buy Uncle Ben's rice and so there is nothing wrong with getting somebody who knows how to sell something.' The 'something' that Beers is selling is 'an elegant brand' called 'the US' and the President and Secretary of State are the 'symbols of the brand'.[1] Beers told *Business Week*: '[T]he whole idea of building a brand is to create a relationship between the product and its user. ... We're going to have to communicate the intangible assets of the United States – things like our belief system and our values.'[2]

But there is already a well established 'relationship' between 'the product and its user': a relationship based on half a century of experience of how corporate America has sold itself to the rest of the world. One outcome of the spread of American hamburgers throughout the globe, and the philosophy associated with them, is that it has spread standardisation throughout the world. A Big Mac is made by the same process, packaged in exactly the same containers, weighs the same, and is sold in the same way in similar restaurants throughout the world. There may be regional variations to capture the local palate and cultural imagination – Curry Burgers in India, Samurai Burgers in Japan, Rendang Burgers in Malaysia and Indonesia – but the product is the same, despite its McDonaldised 'diversity'. This is exactly what the rest of the world has experienced from American foreign policy: with the US you get a standardised theory and practice in its dealings with the world. The theory is always about 'our values', which are placed on a global pedestal: justice, democracy, human rights, freedom, civic concerns, compassion, resolve, responsibility – all the great virtues of Western civilisation. But the practice consistently contradicts these values. In other words, politically, America relates to the rest of the world in terms of double standards. This is one of the most common complaints about America; and a fundamental reason why America is hated in the world.

Consider, for example, the question of justice. The American government proclaims that its system of justice, the law, is at the heart of the nation. It constantly rebukes other nations for being unjust and repressive. In his State of the Union address in February 2002, President Bush declared: 'Our armed forces have delivered a message now clear to every enemy of the United States: even 7,000 miles away, across oceans and continents, on mountain tops and in caves, you will not escape the justice of this nation.' That American foreign policy has its own particular notion of justice became clear when the Pentagon chose 'Operation Infinite Justice' as the original brand name for the bombing war in Afghanistan. As so many Muslims pointed out, according to their beliefs only God, in His Infinite Mercy, can dispense Infinite Justice. Human justice is both finite and fallible. The justice that the rest of the world expected America to implement required the capture of the terrorists, trial in an open criminal court, and then, after a reasoned judgement, a fitting punishment – to be locked up for the rest of their lives. This would not only show what justice is all about, it would also demystify the terrorists, debunk their cause and open the eyes of their followers and supporters. But what did we get instead? 'They don't deserve the same guarantees and safeguards that would be used for an American citizen going through the normal judicial process', declared the Bush administration.[3] Thus, justice for American criminals and terrorists means one thing; but for non-American criminals and terrorists it is quite another thing. A Military Commission would be convened, consisting of a group of officers ordered by the President, their Commander in Chief, to sit in judgement so that the culprits could be 'executed in relatively rapid order'.[4] The Military Commission does not conform to any international notion of justice or fair trial: it violates the fair trial guarantees of the Universal Declaration of Human Rights and the European Convention, and even breaches the minimum requirements of the 1949 Geneva Convention. As a *New York Times* editorial stated, the Military Commission is 'a breathtaking departure from due process'.[5] Geoffrey Robertson QC, one of Britain's most prominent Human Rights lawyers, lists the principal objections to the Military Commission as follows:

1. The commission is not independent or impartial, as required by Articles 84 and 85 of the 1949 Geneva Convention III on the Treatment of Prisoners of War, which the US (and 187 other countries) have ratified. The army officers who will act as 'judges' are paid and promoted by the defence department, an arm of the government which has alleged [the prisoners'] guilt and which acts in any way as their detaining power. These officers are commissioned to sit as 'judges' by the President, the Commander in Chief, who has 'determined in writing' that the defendants should be prosecuted and who thus has a vested interest in their conviction.

2. There is no appeal, except to the President, who cannot be impartial because the decision appealed against is that of his own tribunal.

3. There are no normal evidentiary rules or safeguards – evidence is admissible if the Presiding Officer thinks it should be admitted. A distinguished US judge who made a recent study of the records of military commissions in Japan after

World War II concludes that they 'provide a stark example of the potential for abuse when rules of evidence are so flexible as to be non-existent'.

4. ... The hearing will be in secret and transcripts will not be made available.

5. There is no provision for the burden of proof to be placed on the prosecution, or for it to meet a standard of 'beyond reasonable doubt'. Guilt is simply to be established by evidence 'of probative value to a reasonable person'. The officers who form the 'jury' need not be unanimous – as a vote of two thirds will secure a conviction. They do not give a reasoned written judgement.

6. The sentence of death is traditionally carried out by an army firing squad.[6]

In other words, the Military Commission violates every notion of justice known to civilisation. After accusing the Taliban of violating the basic rules of justice, the US opts to enact justice that is not 'different in essence from the Taliban's football pitch executions'.[7] The Commission cannot even be described as a kangaroo court (an appellation offensive to Australians, who know the loveable qualities of this marsupial) because it is not a court at all: 'It is an extension of the power of the President, who personally or through the officers he commands, acts as prosecutor, judge and jury, and court of appeal judge.'[8]

It is the ostentatious display of such double standards that has made America a global figure of hate. Travel across the world from Brazil to Canada, Pakistan to South Korea, and you will run into huge numbers of people who will, again and again, give the following examples of American double standards.

1. America prides itself on being a democracy, constantly urges

other countries to become more democratic, and censures or takes action against those who, in its government's view, are less than democratic. Yet, American democracy is exceptionally undemocratic. American voters select the most powerful leader in the world, commander in chief of the greatest arsenal of military might ever assembled, and yet the main issue of concern is whether half the electorate will actually bother to exercise this right. What the 2000 Presidential election proved was the lack of trust in direct democracy of the Founding Fathers of America. By design, the American electoral system dictates that the candidate who gains the greatest number of votes from individual Americans across the whole country does not necessarily become President, as happened in the 2000 election. Individual votes are cast not to directly elect the President but to determine the make-up of the Electoral College, apportioned on a state-by-state basis. The number of Electors (the people who form the Electoral College) allocated to each state is proportionate to its population. Different states have different arrangements for the selection of their Electors: in some, candidates get Electors proportionate to their vote; in others, it is winner-take-all. The crucial part of being elected President is building up the right chequer-board of support in particular states. An enormous majority in the popular vote in one particular state, or even a number of states, can be irrelevant to the overall outcome of the election. Where a candidate's supporters live, rather than their absolute number, is what matters. The arcane structure of the electoral process was intended so that in close elections the whole question would ultimately be determined not by the voters but by the voters' representatives, the professional politicians in Congress, although in the 2000 Presidential election, the decision of the Supreme Court – an entirely selected body – abruptly terminated the possible permutations and handed the election to George W. Bush.

2. The US declares that elections should be free and fair, and prohibits other countries from intervening in its own elections,

giving donations to American political parties and influencing the outcome of elections in any way. Yet, it routinely intervenes in the elections of other countries, and funds political parties in developing countries – sometimes covertly through the CIA, at other times through non-governmental organisations and the media. For example, in the 1950s, the CIA provided funds to support the campaign of President Camille Chamoun and selected parliamentary candidates in Lebanon; in the then British Guiana, the US prevented the democratically elected Cheddi Jagan from taking office between 1953 and 1964; in 1966, the CIA funded President René Barrientos of Bolivia to the tune of $600,000 in a successful attempt to influence the outcome of the general election; and in Nicaragua during the 1980s, the US poured in millions of dollars through the National Endowment for Democracy (NED), a specially created front for the CIA, to prevent the Sandinistas from being democratically elected. William Blum, in his book *Rogue State*, provides a list of 23 countries in which the US has 'perverted elections' and interfered with the democratic process to ensure a favourable outcome: Italy 1948–70s, Lebanon 1950s, Indonesia 1955, Vietnam 1955, Guiana 1953–64, Japan 1958–70s, Nepal 1959, Laos 1960, Brazil 1962, Dominican Republic 1962, Guatemala 1963, Bolivia 1966, Chile 1964–70, Portugal 1974–5, Australia 1974–5, Jamaica 1976, Panama 1984, 1989, Nicaragua 1984, 1990, Haiti 1987–8, Bulgaria 1991–2, Russia 1996, Mongolia 1996, Bosnia 1998.[9]

3. The American state sees itself as consistently under threat from 'rogue states' and 'non-state actors'; then there is the 'Russian threat', the 'Chinese threat', the 'Cuban threat', the threat of 'the axis of evil' and the 'terrorist threat'. Yet, militarily, the US is the most powerful country in history, and even if all the other states in the world put all their military resources together they would not be able to mount a credible threat to the US. The colossal US military is more than two-and-a-half

times larger than the militaries of the next nine largest potential adversaries combined: Russia, China, Iran, North Korea, Iraq, Libya, Syria, Sudan, Cuba. There is no equivalent in the world in sheer concentration of power to a US carrier task force: the nuclear-powered carrier group that forms around the USS *Enterprise*, for example, has a combined flight deck almost a mile in length and a superstructure 20 storeys high, and concentrates more military power in one naval group than most developed states can manage with all their armed forces. The US possesses 12 such carriers – with another, the USS *Ronald Reagan*, under development. 'Nothing', writes Paul Kennedy, Professor of History at Yale University, 'has ever existed like this disparity of power; nothing'. The US has accumulated more power than Charlemagne, the Roman Empire, and Britain at its imperial height. Not surprisingly, the US spends more on defence than any other country in history. While the European powers cut their defence spending after the fall of the Berlin Wall, China held its spending in check, and the Russian military budget simply collapsed, the US budget continued to increase from $260 billion in the middle of the 1990s to a staggering $329 billion in 2002. This figure is set to increase to $400 billion – half of all the military spending in the world. And this in a democratic country that claims to despise large government! 'I have returned to all of the comparative defence spending and military personnel statistics over the past 500 years that I compiled in *The Rise and Fall of the Great Powers* [1989], and no other nation comes close', says Kennedy.[10] Despite its unmatched military might and the astronomical figures of its defence budget, money buys insecurity. The US still feels threatened – so much so that it insists on militarising outer space. The US Star Wars programme, aimed at the 'control of outer space', 'domination of outer space' and 'superiority in outer space', envisages deploying space-, land- and sea-based anti-ballistic missile systems, and a variety of orbiting systems that could strike terrestrial targets. Even US arms manufacturers, such as aviation giant Lockheed Martin, are having problems in finding appropriate enemies at which to aim American military might. The French describe US military evolution as *'gigantisme militaire'*, a phrase that incorporates the scale of US military ambition as well as the idea that it is a pathological condition: an organism that has grown so large it is sick.

4. US foreign policy has censored, imposed sanctions on and demonised countries that seek nuclear weapons. It imposed crippling sanctions on Pakistan and India for developing these weapons. It has demonised North Korea for possessing a nuclear arsenal. Yet, it has the world's largest stockpiles of nuclear weapons and is the only country in the world ever to have used atomic weapons (in Hiroshima and Nagasaki) in war. It coerces other countries to sign and ratify, yet has itself single-mindedly refused to sign, the Comprehensive Nuclear Test Ban Treaty. Moreover, it refused to renounce the first-strike use of nuclear weapons or even to commit to refraining from using nuclear weapons against states without nuclear capability. It has even blurred the long-accepted distinction between nuclear and non-nuclear weapons, and foresees the use of nuclear weapons against targets able to withstand attacks by conventional weapons, such as underground bunkers. Furthermore, it is ready to use nuclear weapons on non-nuclear targets such as 'non-state actors', that is, terrorist groups with chemical or biological weapons. While it forces other countries to abandon their nuclear plans, it continues to develop its own programme, developing and designing 'mini-nukes' and restarting nuclear tests. Worse: it unashamedly seeks to claim the moral high ground by suggesting that the new kinds of warheads being developed would actually 'reduce collateral damage'; that is, small nuclear weapons might kill fewer civilians than conventional weapons – an assertion that flies in the face of everything we know about these weapons. The US has contingency plans for nuclear strikes on seven nations – Russia, China, Iraq, North

Korea, Iran, Libya and Syria. All this while, its stated policy remains that of 'negative security assurances' whereby Washington has pledged not to use nuclear weapons against a non-nuclear weapon state unless that state attacks the US or its allies in association with a nuclear weapon state.[11]

5. The United States government demonises and imposes sanctions against other states, such as Iraq, that develop or hold stockpiles of biological and chemical weapons. Yet, it has the world's largest stockpile of smallpox, anthrax, and other biological weapons. It continues to experiment with new weaponised pathogens. It has 30,000 tons of chemical weapons. And it has resolutely refused to support any UN initiative that would ban the development of biological and chemical weapons, or agree to any measures to strengthen a biological weapons treaty.

6. The US government says that it does not kill civilians, and that its 'smart bombs' are aimed only at military targets. Yet, in its role as 'global policeman', it targets civilian infrastructures: water treatment facilities, power plants, dams, flood control systems, irrigation, water storage, pumping stations, medical research centres, baby-food factories, sewage facilities, bridges, transportation facilities, petrochemical plants, fertiliser factories, auto-plants, as well as hospitals, schools, Red Cross buildings, residential neighbourhoods, embassies and, in the Afghanistan war, even a foreign news bureau. In one major campaign lasting over ten years – the Vietnam War – it carpet-bombed three countries (North Vietnam, Cambodia and Laos), killing at least three million civilians. A decade earlier, it carpet-bombed North Korea so thoroughly that it ran out of targets. At the end of the Gulf War, it bombed an Iraqi convoy and buried alive 150,000 conscripts when they had surrendered and were no threat. It promotes the deception that a country can be bombed around the clock with only a few civilian casualties, and then fights to keep the civilian casualties from our television screens.

Just as the US has surpassed all previous empires, such as those of Britain and France, Spain and Portugal, in brute power and confounding hypocrisy, so the hatred for America has far exceeded the scorn thrown at historical imperial powers. The anger directed at the US and voiced from Argentina to Zaire is based on the belief that while its foreign policy demands 'consistency and discipline' from everyone else, America is far from consistent and disciplined itself; while it sells democracy and diversity to the rest of the world, it is in fact deeply undemocratic in its behaviour and deeply intolerant of any state that disagrees with its actions or offers an alternative to Washington's chosen path. The anger and resentment of the rest of the world comes, as Naomi Klein notes in *The Guardian*, 'from a clear perception of false advertising. In other words, America's problem is not with its brand – which could scarcely be stronger – but with its product.' But once a 'brand identity' is established by a corporation,

> it is enforced with military precision throughout a company's operations. The brand identity may be tailored to accommodate local language and cultural preferences (like McDonald's serving pasta in Italy), but its core features – aesthetic, message, logo – remain unchanged. This consistency is what brand managers call 'the promise' of a brand: it's a pledge that wherever you go in the world, your experience at Wal-Mart, Holiday Inn or a Disney theme park will be comfortable and familiar. At its core, branding is about rigorously controlled one-way messages, sent out in their glossiest form, then sealed off from those who would turn corporate monologue into social dialogue.[12]

The 'one-way message' that the US sends out to the rest of the world is that its own cultural and social reality is the only reality that really matters. Just because Americans eat on average three burgers a week (according to *The Dictionary of American*

Slang, the suffix 'burger' means 'any hot sandwich served on a bun, often toasted, with many condiments'), some 38 billion annually, accounting for nearly 60% of all sandwiches eaten in the US – then the rest of the world's people should also eat burgers. Of course, no one forces the rest of the world to eat them – they are undeniably popular – but the desire for American burgers is created through massive advertising, tie-ins with other American cultural products such as Disney films, and their association with the glamour and power of American civilisation itself. And burgers are not just fast food; they are also a fast culture economy. One in ten Americans works for a fast food outlet; and nearly 7% of the US workforce had their first job at McDonald's. If all space is American space, then the cultural space of the globe belongs to the American burger. McDonald's alone has sold 12 hamburgers for every person in the world.

But hamburger chains do not just impose hamburgers on the world. They also carry with them the principles and processes that lie at the base of fast-food restaurants: clinical efficiency, total predictability, callous calculability and complete control through the replacement of human with non-human technology. How could local cultures compete with such an onslaught? To survive, local cultural products have to emulate the imposed American cultural commodities. Local restaurants, for example, end up looking like McDonald's:

> Examples abound including Juicy Burger in Beirut with J.B. the clown standing in for Ronald McDonald and the chain Russkoye Bistro in Russia which is consciously modelled after McDonald's and regards it like a big brother. The most famous restaurant in Beijing – Quanjude Roast Duck Restaurant – sent its management staff to McDonald's in 1993 and then introduced its own 'roast duck fast food' in early 1994. In a sense, it is the largely invisible incursion of the principles of McDonaldisation into local institutions that is a far greater threat to indigenous cultures than the spread

of McDonald's itself (and other American fast food restaurants) to other nations.[13]

In Europe, it is this 'invisible incursion' that has made McDonald's a metaphor for the corrosive influence of American consumer culture, and the most frequent target of local anger and anti-American campaigns. In Britain, for example, a postal worker and a gardener from London (Helen Steel and Dave Morris) took McDonald's to court, alleging that the corporation 'exploits children' with its advertising, is 'culpably responsible' for cruelty to animals, pays its workers exceptionally low wages, and is 'antipathetic' to unionisation. This famous court case, which came to be known as the 'McLibel' trial, ran for two-and-a-half years, becoming one of the longest trials in English history. Giving his verdict on 19 June 1997, the Judge, Mr Justice Bell, ruled that Steel and Morris, who had defended themselves, had indeed libelled McDonald's but that they had also proved many of the allegations. The defendants had shown that McDonald's exploited children, falsely advertised its food as nutritious, risked the health of its long-term customers, and that the corporation was indeed anti-union and cruel to the animals reared for its products. The court case generated immense publicity and led to a huge anti-McDonald's campaign in Britain.

Two years later, on 12 August 1999, José Bové, a French farmer and former union activist, trashed a McDonald's building site in Millau, south-west France. Bové's trial turned into an anti-McDonald's festival: supporters (some on tractors), demonstrators and members of the public turned up to a family day out for all variety of McDonald's-haters. At his trial, Bové said that he objected to the way in which the food sold in McDonald's is farmed, sourced, and processed; he was concerned about the bland homogenisation of culinary culture as represented by the hamburger; and there were community concerns about litter, and the impact of a multinational on local businesses. But more than anything else, he was opposed to the practice of feeding hormones to cattle to artificially speed up their growth. Like the McLibel trial in Britain, Bové's trial gave birth to a major anti-McDonald's campaign in France. Bové himself went on to co-author a best-selling book, *The World is Not for Sale* (2001), which outlines an alternative vision of sustainable and humane farming. He is now regarded as one of the leaders of the international anti-globalisation movement. Anti-McDonald's campaigns, similar to those in Britain and France, can now be found in most European countries.

George Ritzer, Professor of Sociology at Maryland University and author of *The McDonaldization of Society*, argues that American culture has acquired 'obscene power' in the process of replicating itself in the rest of the world. Australian cultural critic and science writer Margaret Wertheim, who lives in Los Angeles, suggests that to much of the rest of the world, 'American culture seems like a virus, a particularly pathological one at that. We might, not without some justification, compare American culture to the AIDS virus, HIV. Like that brilliantly adapted organism, US culture is endlessly self-replicating and alarmingly adept at co-opting the production machinery of its hosts. The reason HIV is so hard to stop is precisely because it harnesses its host's cellular functions, turning the body's power against itself to produce ever more copies of the viral invader. So too, American fast food culture, pop music, films and television infect the cultural body of other nations, co-opting local production machinery to focus their efforts on mimicry. This pattern of viral replication repeats itself the world over, with American pop cultural norms choking out and stifling native flora and fauna.'[14]

The 'virus' of American culture and lifestyle replicates so readily because it is founded on a promise of abundance, the lure of affluence. Material well-being is universally appealing, irresistible to those who have (or are close to having) sufficient means to buy into the dream. It is the upwardly mobile, those busily working to distance themselves from poverty, who find the prospect of ever-expanding material horizons truly intoxicating. There is no mystery, nothing in the least difficult to understand, in this most human of motivations. There is no known human constituency that wishes to vote for poverty. And given the fact that so many people aspire to their lifestyle, it is no surprise that Americans feel that their way is the best and the only way.

The global projection of American affluence, the coded texts of all its popular cultural products, is a permanent advertisement for the goods, services and material endowments that are potentially available, how they can be possessed and how they will make us better, happier, more attractive and more modern. What it costs to acquire this cornucopia is often less apparent. That many of the costs will be intangible – alterations to cherished traditional values and lifeways, undermining of the unquantifiable worth of long-established identities with their sensibilities and refinements – is a pitfall that is never mentioned. What is sold is the prospect of choosing to have whatever one's heart can desire. Everyone believes that sensible choices can and will be made. But that all choices carry unintended, and often undesired, consequences is a realisation that comes after the event. It is a predicament that only gradually became apparent to America and other developed nations. To replicate American abundance – the choice of goods, the service and lifestyle that it permits – does not involve a free choice of means, but adaptation to the constraints of the 'virus': a particular kind of economic organisation, particular political and social forms, that inevitably compromise the 'immune system' of the host. This has been the story of all developed nations, and it did not stop them from seeking more and more abundance. It is the same story for all of the less- and least-developed, and would-be-developing, nations.

'When I was growing up in suburban Australia', says Wertheim, 'America strobed like a lighthouse on our horizon'.

She loved the 'flash and trash' of American culture, epitomised by such sizzling 1960s television shows as the dada spy-spoof *Get Smart* and the subversively feminist *Bewitched*. 'I was entranced; and yet at the same time I felt suspicious of America. Culturally speaking, it was the sixty-pound gorilla in the room; we were bombarded with their films, their television, their music, their celebrities, and their fashions, but ours were utterly invisible to them. A quarter century later, that largely remains the state of affairs', she says. To survive, the Australian film industry started to ape Hollywood. 'This almost proved fatal. In the late 1980s, the Australian film industry almost died after a spate of botched attempts at producing American-style dramas. No one wanted this cynical fare, least of all the Americans at whom these mishmashes were largely aimed.'[15] If the Australian government had not stepped in with state funding, the result could have been devastating. It is not that Australians and New Zealanders in the film industry do not thrive. The current contingent, led by Mel Gibson, Nicole Kidman, Russell Crowe, Cate Blanchett, Baz Luhrman, Peter Jackson, Sam Neill, Peter Weir, Jane Campion and others, all have sparkling careers and notable successes to their names. But their success is found in Hollywood. It comes about by working in the product that Hollywood and its studio production lines determine for the global audience. In order to work they acquire semi-American, vaguely trans-Pacific accents, homogenising out their distinctiveness or subduing it to the imperative for standardisation.

But Australia is not the only nation whose indigenous culture is made invisible and threatened by the juggernaut of American culture. In lobbying for self-protection, French film-makers, for example, understood exactly how powerful the viral agent of American cinema could be. Claudie Ossard, producer of the Oscar-nominated *Amélie*, argues that it will be 'suicidal' for France not to protect its cinema and other cultural products. None of Ossard's films, including such noted works as *Delicatessen* and *Arizona Dream*, could have been made if

French culture were not protected (and films subsidised) by the state. Indeed, the French have been concerned about American-isation since the 1920s and 30s. They were anxious about 'coca-colonisation' (the notion that the threat from the US soft drink symbolised a broader cultural danger), and began to take measures to defend their language, cuisine and art world from American domination. Recent French concerns about, and opposition to, globalisation are based on the same awareness. France knows that a world dominated by the 'free market' is also a world under the tutelage of American culture: that is why 'France is not prepared to sit back and accept all aspects of a globalised, Americanised world. Indeed, it may well be that it is precisely that France is adapting so significantly in the economic domain, where state control is nowhere near the level it was 20 years ago, that the French are all the more determined to pro-tect their culture.'[16]

Both France and Australia are industrial powers and can protect their cultures to some extent. But, as Wertheim asks, 'if rich, white Anglo and European nations feel threatened, how much damage has the onslaught of American cultural hyper-imperialism already done to cultures and peoples of developing countries?'[17] If French film-makers and Australian writers worry about their evolutionary survival, is there any hope for the sur-vival of Third World writers, film-makers and television pro-ducers, or for indigenous cultures and languages?

The simple, and truly frightening, answer is: not much. The ascendancy of the 'hamburger culture' has meant the eradica-tion of indigenous Third World cultures everywhere. Sylvester Stallone, Bruce Willis, Britney Spears, Madonna, Michael Jackson, Jerry Seinfeld and Homer Simpson dominate airwaves and screens the world over. Local products have to compete not only against vast US production budgets – major US studio films now cost well over $100 million, with *Star Wars, Episode One: The Phantom Menace* (1999) coming in at a staggering $115 million, and Michael Jackson's album *Invincible* racking up production expenses of a hitherto unimaginable $30 million (for a single record!) – but also equally lavish promotion budgets. The home-grown culture industries just don't stand a chance. Of course, there are always exceptions to general rules. The Iranian film industry has thrived largely because Hollywood products are not allowed into the country. Bollywood, as the Indian film industry is known, has succeeded by imitating the style and content, and sometimes even the production values, of Hollywood. But these are exceptions, and in any case we are talking about much more than simply film and television, pop music and videos, fast foods and electronic gadgets. In traditional societies of developing countries, identity is shaped by history, tradition, community, ancestors and extended families. American-led globalisation seeks to replace all this with American cultural products. The tsunami of American consumerist culture assimilates everything, exerting immense, unstoppable pressure on the people of much of the world to change their lifestyles, to abandon all that gives meaning to their lives, to throw away not just their values but also their identity, stable relationships, attachment to history, buildings, places, families and received ways of doing and being.

The 'obscene power' of hamburger culture places local cultures in a vice-like grip. American multinationals promote their culture products through a multiple strategy using pop music, local television channels and specially produced style products, thus occupying all available cultural space. Cigarette companies, for example, don't just sell cigarettes: they sell cigarettes as a total style and identity package. The cigarette-hawking cowboy, 'The Marlboro Man', may be under siege back home in the United States, but in Asia it is almost impossible to escape his craggy all-American mug: it is slapped up on billboards, peering through magazines and newspapers, flickering across television screens. He is 'sponsoring' American movies and television series, gazing at everybody in crowded shopping malls, selling 'Marlboro Classic' clothes in shops done up in the style of Wild

West saloons, and enticing the young to smoke in malls and bars where teenage girls, dressed as cowgirls, offer free cigarettes to passing youngsters. Desire is enforced among the young not only to smoke a particular brand of cigarette but also to buy designer clothes stamped with the brand logo ('Salem Attitudes', or 'Pall Mall Action Gear'), shop at the brand's record shops, grace pop concerts sponsored by the brand ('Salem Power' or 'Salem Cool Planet'), and even take a high-concept vacation designed to solve all their identity problems ('Salem Cool Holidays', or 'Mild Seven, or Peter Stuyvesant'). Even those companies that sell nothing but cigarettes promote a packaged identity: in Malaysia, for example, 'Kent Vacations' won't take you anywhere, for despite its heavy advertising presence on the air it doesn't actually exist; and since no one in Kuala Lumpur could work out what 'Benson and Hedges Golden Gallery' actually sold, it has been replaced by a high-concept Bistro hosting regular jazz sessions in which local and American musicians play together. The multitude of style products are used for the construction of images and signs that portray American culture as a bastion of 'freedom' and 'individualism', the only way to be 'cool' or 'hot'. The added seductive pull is the motif 'the consumer is god,' crystallised in the 'American Dream' – sold without irony or doubt. And if there is any doubt, the latest teenage flick from Hollywood playing at the local multiplex will confirm that the American way is the only way to be.

In many developing countries, local television programming has almost been eradicated. This is not because these countries cannot make their own programmes, or that they do not wish to do so; it is largely because the economics of programme-making, combined with the agenda of American multinational advertisers, makes it almost impossible to produce local programmes. Just as America dumps cheap commodities on developing countries, thus forcing locally produced commodities and goods to the wall, so television programmes are dumped on the Third World. The system works like this. A single episode of a hit television show such as *Alias* or *Dark Angel* may cost up to $5 million to make. This money is recouped by selling the show to a single network in the United States and Canada. The European sales are pure profit. Once the American and European markets are sewn up, the programmes are dumped on Third World television stations according to a long-established formula for payment. The higher a country's per capita income, the higher it is on the ladder of 'development', the more it pays. Thus, while a British channel will pay something in the region of £200–250,000 for an episode of a high-rating show like *The Simpsons*, Malaysia may acquire the same show for less than US$70,000 and Bangladesh for only US$25,000. Thus a programme with exceptionally high production values is sold for peanuts, making it impossible for local programming, working on modest to miniscule budgets, to compete. Inevitably, local programming always looks inferior to imported shows. But programmes are not bought individually; they are bought in package deals. So a major proportion of the seasonal output of a local channel in a developing country may consist exclusively of the imported package.

Moreover, each programme of the package will be subsidised or 'sponsored' by a multinational company: the programme will be associated with its name or with one of its brand products. As a general rule, American multinationals do not sponsor local programmes, even if they attract high ratings. They sponsor only those programmes – *Model Inc.*, *Melrose Place*, *Baywatch* – which promote the central images of American culture: the images of high consumption, of unrestrained freedom, of the young individual as the consumer. Thus, television channels in countries with 'open economies', such as South Korea, Taiwan, Malaysia, Singapore, Thailand, Indonesia, Hong Kong, are totally dominated by American companies. These companies also fund frequent 'live concerts' (which come under local programming) in which imported American pop stars entertain the local audience, as well as sports events. When what is being shown on terrestrial television is combined with what is coming down from the satellite – 24-hour MTV, QVC (the 'Quality, Value, Convenience' shopping channel), old American movies on TMC, endless repeats of situation comedies on the Paramount Comedy Channel, and American reality and quiz shows – we get a more accurate picture of the almost total displacement of indigenous culture.

Much the same can be said for the Internet, which was hailed as a great boon for democracy, including cultural democracy (all new technology is initially sold with this false promise). Yet, much of the content is largely controlled by two American giants – AOL Time Warner and Microsoft. Both AOL and Microsoft force their subscribers to remain in their high-pressure bazaars, where their own and their partners' cultural products are hawked night and day. In most Asian middle-class homes, the Internet is accessed through the set-top box and the television screen – all three media are dominated by American multinationals. For example, Robert Murdoch's Star TV, which has almost total control over coaxial cable and satellite, transmits content to around 40 cable channels across Asia. Much of this is American cultural output; and even the Asian material such as pop songs and quiz shows are gaudy imitations of American originals.

The impact of hyper-imperial American culture is not limited to laying waste to indigenous cultures. It also represents an onslaught on indigenous identities. Among Asian youth, for example, the imitation of American culture goes much beyond pop music and designer outfits. Street rappers wearing reversed baseball caps, baggy sweaters and cut-off jeans atop Nike trainers don't merely want to look and sound like disaffected black urban youth in the States – they imbibe the representation of the psychological profile as well. So crime, truancy, drug addiction and promiscuity, along with breakdown of parental authority, are all on the rise in societies in which 'youth' was never a separate concept and the extended family and disciplined personal behaviour were the norm. The most notable feature of this culture of disaffection in Asia is that it is confined to those with the most prolific purchasing power – the children of the privileged, affluent élite. Western pop music, MTV and television programmes, notes *Asiaweek*, 'have created a money minded youth culture that demands instant gratification and thrives on audio-visual bombardment ... [A]s pre-schoolers they start out with Christian Dior sneakers. Then they want *Beverly Hills 90210* spectacles. They even use designer pencil boxes.'[18] But these goods only generate disaffection, for the accent in imported culture is on constant and continuous disaffection. Disaffection is the youth culture of the haves who would like to find meaning in the outrage of the have nots. Thus the interests of affluent youth everywhere in Asia seem to mirror that of the *lepak*, as Malaysia has dubbed its most recently identified social problem – loitering around malls and having all the goods that go with the lifestyle, but a lifestyle in which style is essential to signify meaninglessness, in which a designer fashion-plate is the essence of disaffection. And beyond that lies the flirtation with self-destructive addictive behaviour.

Thus, American-led globalisation uses pop music, television and style products to transform the identity of young people in the developing world into a commodity. The package is sold with the allure of 'freedom'. But this notion of 'freedom' – or more appropriately, libertarian individualism which promotes every individual's potential for fulfilment, the pursuit of endless consumption, the withdrawal of all collective, communal and social responsibility – undermines everything that indigenous cultures, traditions and history stand for.

Local cultural production becomes at best marginalised, at worst totally suppressed. Indigenous music has to be torn away from its context and Westernised to be acceptable to those who are supposed to be its inheritors. Consider, for example, the case of Quawwali, the devotional music of India, Pakistan and Bangladesh. Of mystical Sufi origins, it is sung to the simple rhythm of traditional drums and hand-clapping in praise of

God, Prophet Muhammad, Ali the fourth Caliph of Islam and classical Sufi masters. In its 'new, improved' form, the form in which it has become acceptable to the cool youth of the Subcontinent, it has gone funky and is sung to a syncopated rock beat generated by synthesisers. What was originally designed to induce mystical ecstasy is now used to generate hysteria for rock music and disco dancing. Similarly, Indian film songs, which have traditionally had a high poetic content, now mirror the meaningless lyrics of American pop songs. Given the dominance of English in global cultural products, local languages acquire the image of inferiority. In other words, the production of indigenous culture acquires the sense of backwardness; its themes and concerns are not those to which the growing generation can relate. No wonder the politics of identity has become so important in most of the developing countries.

Languages are, of course, one of the prime tools of cultural expression. So it should not surprise us to discover that the decline of indigenous cultures is also having a serious effect on the languages of the world. Indeed, an indigenous language disappears every two weeks. It is estimated that by the end of the 21st century, 5,500 of the current 6,000 languages now spoken will simply be as dead as Ancient Greek and Latin. Behind each language is a culture, the expressive richness of a living tongue and its infinite capacity to reflect a distinct mode of thought. So, when a language dies, it truly diminishes the capacity of our world to think, to know, to be and to do differently – to be truly other than the dominant culture. As John Sutherland pointed out in *The Independent on Sunday*:

> There is no mystery about the root cause of the linguistic holocaust that we're living through. Take a holiday anywhere in the world. Your airline pilot will, as you listen to the safety instructions (in English), be communicating with ground control in English. Signs in the airport, whatever country you are in, will be duplicated in one of the world's

top twenty languages – mostly likely English. You'll see Coca-Cola logos. MTV will be playing on the screen. Muzak will be crooning Anglo-American lyrics as you walk through the concourse to baggage reclaim. At the hotel, the desk clerk will speak your language, as well, probably, as the bellhop. (His tip depends on being polyglot.) Go to any internet café and the keyboard code that will get you best results is what you are reading now: English – the *lingua franca* of our time … The spread of English is the product of naked linguistic superpower.[19]

Sutherland tell us that a favourite axiom among linguists is: 'A language is a dialect with an army behind it.' Follow the big armies (Roman, Norman, Chinese, Russian) and you will find the 'world languages'. The most potent army, in 2002, flies the stars and stripes. It is not just English, but American, the dominant English dialect, that is killing indigenous languages everywhere. It is a colonialism, notes Sutherland, far more sinister than any practised in history: '[O]nce we just took their raw materials. Now we invade their minds, by changing the primary tool by which they think: "their" language.'[20]

Hamburgers are not just culture and economy – they also entail a location. We can eat them almost anywhere, but most are eaten on the run. Every half a mile or so in the US, one can find a drive-up window ready to sell burgers to people on the move. So there is an architecture and a geographical space associated with burgers. When McDonald's opens a branch in Red Square in Moscow, or the Forbidden City in Beijing, or in the Holy City of Mecca, it changes the architecture as well as the spatial dynamics of the city. The city – any city – is an expression of a culture's values and ideals, hopes and aspirations, social outlook and behaviour. As such, cities are far more than mere form – more than roads and buildings, bricks and mortar; they are images of a society's perception of its destiny. So the appearance of numerous American fast food restaurants in a city transforms the cityscape as well as its inhabitants' perceptions of themselves. American-led globalisation, by imposing a single set of American standards, is increasingly transforming cities of developing countries into monuments to the American will to power. Traditional architecture is bulldozed to be replaced by featureless brickworks, multi-lane roads, shopping malls, hotels and fast food joints. Most cities in the more affluent parts of the Third World either look like Dallas or theme-parked extensions of Los Angeles.

Jeddah in Saudi Arabia, for example, was a historic city with a distinctive character that always impressed visitors. It consisted of a network of remarkable tall houses that made ingenious use of the local meteorological conditions: the uppermost floors were designed to catch the sea breeze, which created upward draughts with regular temperature differentials; the overarching, open, louvered windows filtered out the sun's glare but allowed air to circulate freely in the rooms; the surrounding flat terraces with wooden grilles permitted the movement of any cool air currents on the hottest of summer nights. These traditional houses showed what the power of imagination and craftsmanship in indigenous building could achieve. American influence and big business brought American city planning and architecture to Saudi Arabia; and soon Jeddah became a poor replica of Houston. Narrow streets and alleyways gave way to huge, wide, sun-baked roads and over-heated concrete monstrosities. Traditional architecture, age-old souks, Saudi cafés – all disappeared to be replaced by shopping malls, fast food restaurants, theme parks and hotels. Americanisation has meted out an even worse fate to Mecca, the holiest city of Islam, where there are no streets left for anyone to walk on. American planners, consultants and architects have turned Mecca – which is, of course, the focus for the 1.3 billion Muslims of the planet who face towards the city during their five daily prayers – into a third-rate American city in which tunnels, flyovers, spaghetti junctions and multi-lane motorways compete for attention with gaudy hotels and the ubiquitous shopping malls. The hatred of America that many Saudis exhibit has little to do with the often cited American military presence in 'holy areas' – in fact, American troops are hundreds of miles to the north of what are traditionally considered the holy areas, the cities of Mecca and Medina. It stems more from the fact that the fabric of traditional Saudi life has been torn apart by Americanisation and replaced with centralised, mass-produced monotony. Saudi cities do not reflect the history, culture, tradition or values of the Arabian Peninsula – they sing solemn homilies to the American way of life.

Much the same can be said about many other cities in the developing world. For example, on a visit to Singapore, the cyberpunk author William Gibson found that:

> the sensation of trying to connect psychically with the old Singapore is rather painful, as though Disneyland's New Orleans Square had been erected on the site of the actual French Quarter, obliterating it in the process but leaving in its place a glossy simulacrum. The facades of the remaining Victorian shop-houses recall Covent Garden on some impossibly bright London day ... there was very little to be seen of previous realities: a joss stick smouldering in an old brass holder on the white painted column of a shop-house; a mirror positioned above the door of a supplier of electrical goods, set to snare and deflect the evil that travels in a straight line; a rusty trishaw, chained to a freshly painted iron railing. The physical past, here, has almost entirely vanished.[21]

After America itself, Singapore is perhaps the most pathologically Americanised place on earth, and it represents the future of many Asian and Latin American cities.

Such cultural hyper-imperialism creates a deep strain of hatred for the US, even in countries that are supposed to be close allies. Among the *minjung* (populist) community of South

Korea, for example, abhorrence of American cultural products is intense. The *minjung* consists of a broad alliance of people, including labourers, farmers and the urban poor, who see themselves as stalwarts of traditional Korean culture and who define themselves as victims of US global culture and capitalism. They feel physically, culturally, geographically – and hence psychologically – alienated and dislocated by the Americanisation of South Korea. US-enforced economic policies, such as those we discussed in chapter four, uprooted autonomous *minjung* rural communities, destroyed their traditional lifestyles and forced them to participate subserviently in the maelstrom of Americanised modernity. They believe that Americanisation has produced inequity, exploitation, cultural violence and alienation; and that American culture actually threatens the Korean language itself, which, some suggest, may die off in the next three decades. Indeed, they consider the US to be an occupying power, and are disgusted at the presence of 45,000 American troops on their soil for over five decades. Hardly surprising, then, that they demonstrate against the USA, and burn the stars and stripes, with seasonal regularity.

'It will be wrong', says Steve Fuller, the American academic who occupies the Chair of Sociology at the University of Warwick, 'to think of American-led globalisation as a form of cultural imperialism. The idea of cultural imperialism implies a much more planned and directed impact on the native culture – what used to be called "ideological warfare", in which people are explicitly told, or forced, to give up their traditional customs and adopt Western ones. But this is not really America's style. Indeed, unlike European cultural imperialism, the US government is rarely directly involved in the most pervasive forms of cultural terrorism, such as McDonaldization.' The desirability of American cultural products – which are perceived to be superior, modern, the wave of the future – means that the 'victims' themselves play an important role in the spread of American culture. Fuller suggests that to really understand what America is doing to the rest of the world, we need to think of US cultural practices in terms of 'bioterrorism', which is almost the exact opposite of the classical form of warfare and cultural imperialism.

> First, [bioterrorism] has no clear goal or point. One does not win a bioterrorist campaign: one simply hopes that the spread of the germ or virus will be as disruptive to society as possible. This may then lay the condition for achieving some other goal. Second, the bioterrorists themselves only start the campaign. Most of the actual 'warfare' is conducted by the victims themselves, who infect each other with the germ or virus in their day-to-day interactions. Third, as the bio-terrorist campaign spreads, and the effects of the germs and viruses are combined with other effects, it becomes virtually impossible to find any single responsible agent, since by that point almost all the victims have become complicit in its spread.
>
> McDonald's illustrates this sense of cultural terrorism beautifully. Consider the sign in front of every Golden Arches: 'Billions served'. Notice it is not: 'Billions fed'. From a marketing standpoint, this is a very striking slogan. It points to no goal other than the proliferation of burgers, and it makes no reference to the response of those to whom the burgers are served. But, as we know, the proliferation of burgers has had a devastating effect on most of the world – from forcing the natives to adopt the practices of American culture to blighting their cultural and physical landscapes. In fact, when the natives start behaving more like the burger giants, and start infecting themselves with their attitudes and behaviour (impatience, obesity, heart disease etc.), they become even more susceptible to even more American inter-ventions. By the time serious damage has been done, enough of the natives will have personally benefited from the inter-vention that it will be very difficult to undo.[22]

While the 'biological terrorism' of the ubiquitous hamburger culture has reduced the cultural geography of the world to a totalising American space, killing the languages, architecture, film industries, television programming, music and art of most of the developing world, American cultural space itself is free from all 'contamination'. The 'free trade' in the cultural sphere is purely one-way. Try getting an Iranian film or a Chinese television series released in the US. Even the best British, Canadian and Australian films – which share the same language and much of the same cultural history – hardly ever play in more than a few art-house cinemas Stateside. With the odd very rare exception, US network television screens nothing but US products. Only on cable channels such as the Sundance and Independent Film Channels will foreign films be found, with British dramas and documentaries occasionally screened on PBS. 'If something truly irresistible turns up from a foreign land, the standard American response is to buy up the rights and remake it in a US version', says Margaret Wertheim. That is what happened with the hit television series *Survivor*, a concept that originated in the Netherlands, and the British hit comedy *Absolutely Fabulous*, whose remake rights were bought up by Roseanne Barr. These are but the latest examples. Britain's groundbreaking 1960s situation comedy *Till Death Us Do Part*, the original socialist/liberal versus conservative/reactionary satire, became the much more affectionate world of *Archie Bunker* once translated across the Atlantic. Films that have suffered this ignominious fate include Wim Wenders' delicate *Wings of Desire*, remade as the saccharine *City of Hope* starring America's sweetheart Meg Ryan, and the brilliant French Comedy *Les Visiteurs*, bizarrely remade by Hollywood with the same two French actors but with the women from the French version replaced by American actresses half their age. In both cases, the Hollywood version was a pale and powerless reflection of the European original. 'The American repackaging machine reduces all experiences, no matter what their cultural context, to American experience', Wertheim notes.[23]

The cut-throat commercialism of the American media enshrines the conventional wisdom of giving the people the lowest common denominator. A country of continental proportions with a population of over 250 million, America clearly sustains specialist audiences with specialist tastes. But mainstream media in prime-time venerates the mass audience, and the production decisions that it makes reflect a market-tested idea of what Americans want to know about the world. One piece of conventional wisdom is that without the presence of an American, the world is essentially uninteresting. The standard practice has long been to cast an American star in a leading role. But increasingly it has come to mean adapting stories to incorporate an American perspective, even when this makes nonsense of the story being told. For example, in 2001 the Hallmark channel broadcast a TV mini-series of the classic 16th-century Chinese novel, *Journey to the West*, an allegorical fable about a real journey to India, made in the 7th century, in search of Buddhist scriptures. For television, according to Hallmark's publicity material, Wu Ch'eng-En's story has been 'updated and modernized'. This is achieved by inserting a new 'dashing hero', a contemporary American 'China-scholar-turned-business-consultant', who has been recognised by the Terracotta Warriors as 'The Scholar from Above' and charged with the heroic task of finding the manuscript in three days or facing 'the world's end'. In this revision, the new hero is accompanied by the story's original hero, The Monkey King, who teaches him the noble skills of martial arts while learning 'something of the human heart'.[24]

It is not only literature that must be rendered into American terms and made palatable to US audiences and their sensibilities. History must also be subjected to the same procedure. The 1995 film *A Little Princess* manages to do both simultaneously. Frances Hodgson Burnett's classic children's book, originally written in 1888 and rewritten in 1905, is the tale of the daughter of a British officer in the Indian Army. Deposited at a boarding school, she goes from riches to rags and learns the meaning of poverty. The film version resets the story in 1914, when the father must go off to the war in the trenches. But somehow his daughter – who has been raised exclusively in India, where she managed to acquire an American accent – is sent to school in New York. On arriving there, she finds that the son of the old gentleman next door is tearfully being sent off to war too – an event that, had it happened in reality, would have caused a riot, since in 1914 America was at the height of its isolationism and determined not to be drawn into a European war.

War is one of the main arenas in which American films routinely re-imagine or distort history. European audiences may have been moved by Steven Spielberg's meticulous recreation of the horrors of the Normandy landings in *Saving Private Ryan* (1998), but they were incensed that at no stage did the film acknowledge that any other nationality participated in the war against Hitler. The insularity that was once an American political stance has become a cultural cocoon in which the rest of the world exists to provide backdrops for American heroics and to supply the villains whom the US must overcome. In *The Patriot* (2000), Mel Gibson's epic of the American Revolutionary War, the British troops are reconstructed as veritable Nazis, committing atrocities relocated from World War II.

Thus, while the rest of the world is suffocating under the weight of American cultural products, Americans themselves are totally insulated from non-American cultures. 'The musical scene is almost as uniform as its televisual cousins – an unbroken vista of American pop, hip-hop and country broken only by the occasional breakthrough of a big British band. Mention Om Kalsoum, the transcendent Egyptian singer beloved throughout the Arab world or Lata Mangashtar, the Indian female vocalist who has sold more records than anyone ever, including Michael Jackson and the Beatles, and the average American music lover will stare in blank incomprehension', says Wertheim.[25] Of course, this situation is not restricted to America – it is symptomatic of a more general problem in the West as a whole, where there is little awareness of non-Western arts and cultures. But America seems worse because it is in a dominant position to *export* its culture – and it is, moreover, as ignorant of European culture as it is of any other.

This is one reason why many Americans cannot imagine the depths of resentment they evoke. As Wertheim notes: '[T]hey seem not to be able to imagine life itself in any guise other than the one they themselves are enmeshed in. And how could they, when their cultural landscape is so thoroughly mono-toned? It is quite unrealistic to expect that someone brought up on a diet of exclusively American media should comprehend the dynamics of Arab culture or appreciate the struggle needed to survive in an African village. If we have here a failure of the collective American imagination, that lack has at least some of its roots in the abject failure of the American cultural production industries which resolutely refuse to open their doors to anything foreign.'[26] In short, Americans themselves become the victims of, and are strangulated by, American cultural hyper-imperialism.

The question thus arises: if the majority of Americans are ignorant of other cultural possibilities and modes, are they therefore innocent of their own culture's increasingly virulent hyper-imperialism? What, then, of US innocence? Are US citizens any more culpable than HIV, a wholly insentient life form? Can the ignorance of American citizens of the bioterrorism of their culture be excused? Ignorance here is essentially wilful. As Margaret Wertheim points out: '[T]oo few Americans seem to want to know about other cultural options; too few are prepared to engage with other people's choices, others' ways of being. In the land of the free, the underlying ethic of too much discourse is that one is free only to do things "our way". As Henry Ford said of his motor car: "You can have it in any colour you like as long as it's black." In this case, of course, the singular option is white. Ignorance may be bliss – though in the wake of 9-11 even that old faith has been called into question. As American-led globalisation decimates the cultures of the world, the responsibility rests with American citizens to preserve what we might call cultural biodiversity. American citizens can no more evade that responsibility and retain moral integrity than they can evade their duty to participate in preserving actual biodiversity. Continued evasion can only result in more hatred abroad and more retaliation at home.' [27]

Even in burger heaven, there is more than one way to grill ground beef patties. The first Wimpy Burger appeared in 1934. Named after the hamburger-eating character in the children's cartoon *Popeye*, this burger offered a sit-down dining experience and went for more sophisticated patrons who could pay the upmarket price of ten cents a burger. Moreover, it refused, with dogmatic determination, to follow other burger outlets with the advent of the drive-in in the late 1930s. A Wimpy experience just could not be had if the diners were allowed to remain in their cars. But Wimpy did more than simply stand up to the concept of drive-in service that became the mainstay of the American fast food industry. Its founder realised he had created a potent virus. In keeping with his wishes, all 1,500 Wimpy Burger restaurants, in the US and other parts of the world, were closed down when he died in 1978.[28]

CHAPTER FIVE

American Stories and Telling Stories to America

Events of enormity are a public trauma, an assault on the collective psyche. They demand public memorials, public words, signs and symbols. When he addressed a joint session of Congress on 20 September 2001, President George W. Bush observed: 'Americans are asking, why do they hate us?' He provided a direct answer: 'They hate our freedoms – our freedom of religion, our freedom of speech, our freedom to vote and assemble and disagree with each other.' America had awakened to danger and was called to defend freedom, he said, and 'whether we bring our enemies to justice or justice to our enemies, justice will be done'. In his first televised address on 9-11, Bush had provided the same answer in words that recall the aspirations of the first settlers: 'America was targeted for attack because we're the brightest beacon for freedom and opportunity in the world. And no one will keep that light from shining.' Furthermore, he declared in his annual speech to Congress that the State of the Union was evident in the nation's response to 9-11: rescuers working beyond exhaustion, the unfurling of flags, the decency of a loving and giving people. And America was touched by seeing the members of Congress gathered on the steps of the Capitol Building on the evening of 9-11, joined in singing 'God Bless America'.

In rhetoric and symbols it is the *idea* of America, America's idea of itself, that has been at the centre of national consciousness since the events of 11 September. Love of one's homeland is not unique to America, nor is it to be derided. What is at issue is how this sense of identity is employed to limit or act as a substitute for political debate about the policies and actions taken in the name of the nation at home and abroad.

No nation is more replete with patriotic imagery in word, song and symbol than America. No nation makes more use of its icons to express an idea of self that is explicitly a view of history, of society and of national mission. American rhetoric and the American narrative tradition are shaped by a mythic vision, one consciously created, diligently taught, incumbent upon new citizens who would be Americans. At a crucial period in the making of modern American society, this mythic vision and the ethos it contains found expression in cinema. The point was made by Frank Pierson, President of the Academy of Motion Picture Arts and Sciences, in his speech to the 2002 Oscar awards ceremony. In the early years of the 20th century, he said – when the largest influx of immigrants were in the process of becoming Americans – silent movies provided a common cinematic language for a population that did not yet speak English. He could have added that the movies acquainted them with the mythic vision, the fund of stories and their encoded values, the idea of America. Through movies and television, America has not only told the stories that form its own mythic vision, but also exported them to the rest of the world through its dominance of global popular culture and entertainment. The whole world is familiar with the idea of America and the American idea of self. Yet far from providing what Pierson called a 'universal language' for discussion of what matters, the American myth works to circumscribe debate, create opposition and fuel antagonism.

Moreover, from outside America, from the perspective and with the historical experience of the rest of the world, the orthodox American narrative reads very differently. Instead of confirming America as the last best hope of mankind, it reveals America as the prime mover and chief beneficiary of the processes that create and sustain a world of haves and have nots, of heard and unheard, of masters and dependants, rulers and ruled. Through the eyes and experiences of developing countries, there is more to the American story than its mythic vision acknowledges. American belief in its own national myth as a model for all nations became a major factor on the world stage in the aftermath of World War II. This single-minded, monolithic outlook was received as something other than simple altruism. America's stance towards the rest of the world appeared as a new imperialism, different but not distinct from the varieties of imperialism that have been distorting the aspirations of three-fifths of humanity for centuries. Indeed, as an accumulation of all previous imperialisms, the pursuit of the American dream as a global dispensation laid the basis for hyper-imperialism, in which America subsumed the rest of the world as its own backyard, to be known and engaged with in purely American terms.

The uses of history and the arrogant recourse to mythic ideals as fact, as much within America itself as in American policy towards the rest of the world, are the substantive political issues that must be debated. When criticism of the US is marginalised, denounced and vilified within America, is it any wonder that it is taken as aggressive posturing without? Or as Lewis Lapham, Editor of *Harper's Magazine*, put it in 1997:

I wonder how a society can long endure by defining truth as the acceptance of untruth, or by passing legislation incapable of being enforced, or by thinking that freedom is a trust fund inherited at birth and certain to last a lifetime ...[1]

The price of freedom is eternal vigilance, an aphorism most

often used to empower the national security state and its foreign policy, and thereby compound the problem. Another kind of vigilance is needed that does not foreclose self-reflection and debate about the failures of real freedom and the abuses of it. It is not love of home or allegiance to identity that is the problem, but the narrow orthodoxy of a particular vision of patriotism, intolerant of self-criticism, devoid of reflection, closed to alternative and diverse interpretation. Dr Samuel Johnson famously noted in 1775, on the eve of the American Revolution, that patriotism is the last refuge of the scoundrel. The American heretic Ambrose Bierce begged to differ – it is, he said, the first. And there is, as the English novelist Mrs Gaskell noted, that kind of patriotism which consists in hating all other nations. Then there is that kind of patriotism which sees all other nations as either failed examples of what a nation should be, or inferior and incapable examples desperately in need of remedial education. The more uncritical the kind of patriotism that rules popular imagination and public discourse, the more alone, insulated, special and different the American ethos makes people feel. The more it holds up a distorting mirror to itself and the rest of the world, the more incomprehensible the rest of the world becomes, full of inarticulate, hostile elements, true barbarians. The term 'barbarian' originated among the Ancient Greeks. To Greek ears, foreign languages sounded like 'ba-ba'. The word came to refer to anyone incapable of speaking Greek, and carried the implication that barbarism was a defect of reason. Not a bad metaphor for how the rest of the world conceives – with justification – that America thinks of itself: as the type site of all that is reasonable and good, while all others are incomprehensible barbarians who just will not see what's best for them.

What the rest of the world sees of America in action at home and abroad is so contradictory to this ideal mythic vision that it inevitably prompts questions. Why do the nation's inherent flaws, the failures to live out or up to its ideals, not ruffle the self-assurance of Americans? Why, in the face of any issue or crisis, does political discourse fall back upon affirming the fundamental perfections of the idea of America as immutable givens? Far from expanding to take up the freedoms that their nation proclaims Americans are heir to, the terms of political debate appear to be narrowing and making more and more insistent references to the orthodox national myth and its ethos.

The American story is myth in the precise sense of the term. Myths are stories concerned with origins or the creation of some phenomenon that is social rather than individual. The American mythic vision is a set of connected motifs: from taming the wilderness and settling the frontier, the quest for freedom, the rugged individualism and self-reliance of those who created the nation, to establishing the perfect union and enshrining self-evident truths and living out a 'manifest destiny'. The American narrative tradition embodies this mythic vision as morality tales in which the idea of America is pure and perfect and the American self is innocent and good. It is the burden, for example, of Frank Capra's film *Mr Smith Goes to Washington* (1939), in which an innocent belief in the purity of American democracy wins out over corrupt politicians and cynical journalists, thanks to the inherent goodness of Mr Smith.

There is, within this mythic tradition, a contradiction created by selective reading of history. The authorised selections are branded as the only facts. The more these facts are questioned, the more resolute the defence of the myth, the more polarised society becomes. We can see this in the American debate on multiculturalism, the most contested arena of which has been education – and in particular the development of Afrocentric education. Black Americans have argued that being educated in the Western canon not only perpetuates social exclusion but continues the fiction that blacks have been marginal to the history and growth of America. In order to develop a new, empowered sense of self-worth, new curricula are needed that reflect black experience and incorporate learning about African roots and African cultural achievement. Opponents argue that this dilutes 'real' civilisation, since the Western canon represents the greatest and most enduring repository of human intellectual and artistic achievement, and that it should therefore be obligatory for study. Afrocentric education, its critics argue, substitutes the study of inferior cultural artefacts and ideas that have not contributed to the rise of civilisation, as well as offering an equally mythic and romanticised notion of Africa.

At home, in a nation of immigrants, the multiculturalism debate goes directly to the meaning of identity, the nature of the mould used to create the character called an American. In the global context, the debate bears on the question of the kind of relationships possible in a world that has for centuries been shaped by Western dominance. Western civilisation constructed not only terrestrial empires and colonies but also an intellectual empire in which it alone exemplified the proper meaning and use of reason, objectivity and adherence to universal concepts and principles, the routine procedures of its disciplines of knowledge. Therefore, Western civilisation has always known the reality, history and ideas of other civilisations better than they have known themselves. By definition, then, other societies and their cultural manifestations are not universal, and to make them the basis of modern education is to depart from the path of human progress and debase the currency of education.

For America, the multicultural debate seems like a fight for survival, and that's the essence of the problem. If freedom, liberty and justice have not been pure, perfect and good in practice – either in history or in contemporary society – then America is not innocent and virtuous, neither special nor different, not the last best hope but just like all other societies, another flawed human endeavour saddled with imperfections that has to face up to the challenge of change.

The US culture wars, the acrimonious bifurcation of liberal and conservative outlooks, began with the rise of a dissident counter-culture in the domestic turmoil caused by the Vietnam War in the late 1960s. It is the liberal and counter-cultural ethos that also motivates the multicultural debate, and both movements are concerned with what it is permissible to believe as true about the origins and social order of America. It is a bitter battle that has created fault-lines in politics, academia and popular debate. Increasingly, it has come to be a battle between orthodoxy and civic heresy that demands taking sides rather than reflecting on the questions or taking a self-critical look at alternative possibilities. What would be the consequence of a critical self-examination? It might explain how the rest of the world thinks about America, why people consider America's claims about itself to be contradictory and unconvincing, why America is seen as central to the global problems between the West and the Rest, and why American intransigence fuels irritation, frustration and hostility the world over. In short, it might open the question of why people hate America to debate, rather than inciting the discourse of the 'bomb-o-gram', the quaint slang used by American servicemen for the carpet-bombing of Vietnam, whose significance we will examine in the next chapter.

Read from the perspective of the Third World, the origins of America are not at all mythic. The origins of America begin with the ideology that bred imperialism. The creation of America is one branch of the familiar story of the rise of Western power that began with the expansion of Europe. So, let's take a brief detour to the origins of European imperialism to see how it became the foundation for American hyper-imperialism.

European expansion was a conscious undertaking. It had a rationale and a justification shaped by the history, ideas and identity of Western Christendom. These are set out explicitly in the series of Papal Bulls and charters that licensed the so-called 'voyages of discovery'. They show that the basic premise of Western expansionism was an oppositional ideology of its own superiority, and superior right, and the enduring otherness, difference and inferiority of the Rest. These documents justified Europe's right to attack, appropriate and possess lands and peoples who, from their own perspective, had every right to believe they were the owners of their own land, property, persons and destiny. This process, once begun, leads inevitably to imperialism in all its guises, and continues to operate in the hyper-imperialism of America today.

Dum Diversas is the earliest in the series of Papal Bulls, granted to the Portuguese monarch in 1453. Its language and ideas were used by all European nations who sponsored expansionary enterprises. *Dum Diversas* authorised the King of Portugal to attack, conquer and subdue 'Saracens', pagans and other unbelievers who were inimical to Christ; to capture their goods and their territories; to reduce their persons to perpetual slavery; and to transfer their lands and properties to the King of Portugal and his successors. Similar Bulls were granted to the Spanish monarchs Ferdinand and Isabella before Columbus set sail. The same terms appear in the Charter granted by Henry VII of England to John Cabot in 1482 before his voyages exploring North America, the basis for all subsequent English claims to what became the United States. The Cabots were licensed to occupy and set up the King's banners and ensigns 'in any town, city, castle, island or mainland whatsoever, newly found by them', anywhere in the 'eastern, western or northern sea', belonging to 'heathens and infidels, in whatsoever part of the world placed, which before this time were unknown to all Christians'. The Charter empowered them 'to conquer, occupy and possess' all such places, on condition of paying the king 'the fifth part of the whole capital gained' in every voyage.

The concerted effort by European nations to 'discover' new territory was not an exercise in scientific curiosity. It was a pragmatic response to an old problem, the geo-political problem that shaped European identity, developed a European sense of mission and had posed an economic dilemma for Europe since the 8th century. When Columbus presented his novel plan to find the East, the land of Cathay, by sailing westward, he was, in his own mind, hoping to open a new front in a seventh Crusade and, as frequently mentioned in his own writings, make possible the recapture of Jerusalem. The so-called 'Age of Discovery' was a strategic manoeuvre in the continuing power rivalry between Christendom and Islam. This struggle has many parallels with the Cold War, and it forged the ideas and attitudes that became fundamental to the making of America.

Like the Cold War, the power struggle between Christendom and Islam was ideological. It was not inevitable, not based on something inherent in religion, either Christianity or Islam, *per se*. It was a product of Christian ideas and outlook based on a particular understanding of religion at a particular time in history. This ideological 'Hot War' was long, bloody and brutal, and gave birth to the black arts of propaganda to support and sustain the military expeditions known as the Crusades and the Reconquista. For Europe, it shaped an understanding of the world rooted in enduring enmity based on ideology. All ideological systems produce a distinction between 'Them' and 'Us'. The ideological underpinnings of the Cold War of the 20th century were a definition of differences in ways of life, principles and values, organisation of economy, society and politics. Things were no different in the earlier era of power rivalry. In the Hot War, all of these differences were seen as natural outcomes of difference in religion.

The founding event of this geo-political outlook was the Battle of Tours in France in 732 AD. There, the army of the Franks led by Charles Martel – Charles the Hammer – turned the tide of Muslim expansion. It was a European victory, the army opposing the Muslims being described as 'the Europeans' in contemporary records. It was thus in opposition to Islamic civilisation that medieval European society took shape. Medieval Christianity formed a total society – one might say a totalitarian society. The first rite of the Church, baptism, made a child both a true human being and a member of civic society, a citizen. Orthodox belief was the definition of the good citizen. The boundaries of citizenship were defined by heresy, a crime against religion that was investigated by the Church but punished by secular rulers. To be an orthodox Christian was the necessary precondition for making society in all its legal, political and social dimensions possible.

Europe lived and developed within a war psychosis, conscious of an enemy with whom it was not evenly matched. Weak and divided Europe faced an adversary that was intellectually, culturally, economically and militarily more advanced. The sudden upsurge of the Muslim Empire was inexplicable to Europe. From the perspective of Christianity, what need was there for a new religion when the Son of God had already died for man's sins? The polemic tradition of reporting on Islam begun by John of Damascus (d. 748 AD) portrays it as an anti-religion, brutal, demonic, libidinous and abandoned, fanatic and implacably opposed to all the norms of the Christian life. John of Damascus essentially 'dismissed Islam as a religious fraud devised from the beginning to facilitate aggression and lust'[2] by presenting it as something it could not be, indeed could easily be known not to be. In his book *Heroes and Saracens*, as we saw in chapter two, Norman Daniel describes this attitude as 'knowledgeable ignorance', and it was used strategically for propaganda purposes. John of Damascus' crude stereotypes had an enduring impact on Western learning and cultural products. 'The earliest Christian reactions to Islam were much the same as they have been until quite recently. The tradition has been continuous and it is still alive', says Daniel.[3] This tradition has come to be known as Orientalism, and is diagnosed today as Islamophobia: 'an irrational hatred and fear of Islam and Muslims'.[4] Daniel argues that Salman Rushdie's novel *The Satanic Verses* (1988) is a contemporary example of this tradition. 'The style of the day changes, but the themes are perennial', he says.[5]

The life of the Muslim world became known to Europe as opulent, provided with technological sophistication, scientific learning, literary and philosophic achievement and a cornucopia of resources far beyond anything available in the West. To acquire these goods and techniques, Europe was dependent on trade with its adversary. The terms of medieval trade were hugely weighted in favour of the Muslim world, and acquiring the gold to pay for these goods only added to the problem. The gold came from West Africa along the Muslim trans-Saharan trade routes to the Maghrib, the region of present-day Morocco, Algeria and Tunisia, from where it was traded to Europe. It then circulated around Europe before flowing out again in trade with the Muslim ports of the Levant, the eastern Mediterranean terminals of the Muslim-dominated trade routes which stretched to the Spice Islands of the Indies and China in the Far East.

The Crusades began on 27 November 1095, when Pope Urban II preached at Clermont in France. In both surviving accounts of this sermon, by Robert the Monk and Fulcher of Chartres, the Pope describes the enemy in familiar ideological terms: 'a despised and base race, which worship demons'; 'an accursed race'; 'unclean nations'. The enemy was, supposedly, attacking Christians in the Middle East, throwing them off their lands, despoiling and destroying Christian altars, appropriating churches for the rites of their own religion. In Robert the Monk's version, the Pope presents the Crusade as the special mission of the Franks, the French people, and also an opportunity for this special people to escape the confines of lands 'too narrow for your large population'. Europe, Urban argued, was riven by conflict within. It was right that Europeans should turn from this sinful rivalry to their proper mission by attacking the pagans and infidels. The Crusade would be a Holy War in two senses: it would be for the advance of Christian society; and it would be an armed undertaking that would earn the expiation of sins for all who took part. Those who took the Cross, becoming Crusaders, would be set on the road to Paradise. This conflict was steeped in history, 'a war that should have been begun long ago'.

The Crusades are not five or six separate events – they are an era, a set of ideas, the context that shaped five centuries of European history. A view of the world is more than politics and law; it finds expression in all the cultural products of a civilisation, and the Crusading ideal shapes the narrative tradition found in the popular literature of all European languages: the romances of chivalrous knights 'doing what a man's got to do'. The Crusades were not simply foreign military expeditions external to Europe – they were also *internalised* as a view of the world. Moreover, the conflict was conducted within areas that we now think of as Europe. Spain and Portugal were alternative areas of Crusading, as was Eastern Europe. When Charles Martel turned the tide, most of the Iberian Peninsula, present-day Spain and Portugal, was part of the Muslim Empire. The Moorish kingdoms of Spain became a major route through which the learning, technology and resources of Muslim civilisation passed into Europe – everything from philosophy to scientific discoveries, paper-making and windmills to sugar and spices. If the territory of the Muslim Empire defined the boundary of Europe, the frontier was in Spain. The Spanish frontier was the Wild West of its day, territory that attracted the equivalent of hired guns, the knights who came from all across Europe. That, as Terry Jones has pointed out, is part of the satire in Chaucer's *Canterbury Tales* (c.1387). Among the group of pilgrims that Chaucer describes is a 'very parfait gentle knight', but the list of his exploits includes some notoriously violent actions, in Spain and also on the eastern frontier. The object of the violence was to win territory from the infidel enemy, land that would then be made safe by a new settler population who would tame what had been the wild dividing line between civilisation and its adversary.

Medieval Christianity defined the identity of Europe, and in so doing produced a clear definition of who and what was the Other: the unbaptised, non-Christians. But not all other people were the same. St Thomas Aquinas defined two basic categories: the vincibly and invincibly ignorant. The vincibly ignorant were those Others who had knowledge of Christianity but had consciously rejected inclusion. As clearly set out in Canon Law, this group comprised Jews and Muslims. Jews were the Other who existed within the boundaries of Christian society, discriminated against and persecuted for their otherness. Muslims were the Other without, people not expected to exist within European society. The invincibly ignorant were those Others who had never encountered the message of Christianity. These were the distant peoples who lived beyond the encircling Muslim lands, only vaguely known from the writings of classical antiquity, but who could be converted, made subject to the polity of Western Christendom. The invincibly ignorant were barbarians, and included savages – people who could legitimately be enslaved. (The institution of slavery was a survival from Roman times that never fully disappeared from medieval Europe. The word 'slave' derives from 'Slav', referring to the Slavic peoples of Eastern Europe.) Among this second category of the invincibly ignorant, Europe hoped to find allies in its battle against Islam. If only it could find a way to circumvent the Muslim lands.

Finding a way around the lands of Islam would also open direct access for trade in all those goods from the 'Indies' that were becoming staples of European life. It would undercut the economic strangle-hold that Muslim civilisation had over Europe. When the Crusades faltered in their objective of securing a European presence in the Middle East, the venture of exploration began in earnest. In 1492, a few days after the completion of the Reconquista – the reconquest of all Spain, achieved with the fall of the last Muslim sultanate, Granada – Their Most Catholic Majesties, Ferdinand and Isabella, summoned Christopher Columbus and finally gave their approval for his novel proposal to continue the Crusade against the infidel, seeking the East by sailing westward across the Atlantic.

Columbus set sail armed with conventional European learning and ideas. His proposal to sail west was inspired by a newly reprinted error, the under-calculation of the circumference of the Earth by the ancient Greek scholar Ptolemy. Columbus travelled with a set of books containing the repository of contemporary European ideas about the world and its peoples; and he is credited with finding a 'New World', despite his own insistence that he had actually arrived in the Far East. Yet it was old ideas that Europe used to make sense of this newness. The Europeans who settled the newly found continent brought with them the motifs, ways of thinking and self-perceptions of Western Christendom. In this new location, old ideas and reflexes began a new career of colonial domination.

In the wake of Columbus, Europeans could claim to have advanced beyond the learning of Ancient Greece, Rome, the Fathers of Christianity, and also the learning of Islamic, Hindu and Chinese civilisations. The Ancients and the Fathers of Theology had insisted that the 'antipodes' could not be peopled, that human life was impossible in the torrid zones of the globe. In their Age of Discovery, contemporary Europeans proved them wrong. Practical knowledge, the information gathered by seamen and travellers, played a major part in shaping the new scientific outlook that was emerging in Europe, and when this was used to investigate the world afresh, a different picture of the East could be presented. Reports by travellers, traders and emissaries regularly stated that while Europeans were advancing in learning, the Orient was atrophied, decaying, falling back on superstition. It might once have been more sophisticated, more scientifically and technologically adept, but that was a thing of the past. The Orient was forever stalled, its development arrested, and the main reason for its decay was continued adherence to the wrong religion. The torch of civilisation, of reason and scientific understanding, the mantle of innovation, the mission of Christianity, had moved west. It had been taken up by new hands, those of the European nations who were pushing the boundaries of Europe ever outward.

The single generation from 1492, when Columbus made landfall on Hispaniola, to 1526, when Ferdinand Magellan completed the first circumnavigation of the Earth, was momentous for Europe. Not only were all the old textbooks rendered incomplete by the new discoveries, but the way in which

Europeans thought about this information, what it meant in terms of the origins and purpose of the world, was reformulated. In one generation, two quantum leaps occurred. As knowledge of the terrestrial world was expanding, so the spiritual world was undergoing a Reformation. The new reformed religion provided new authority for individuals to search and inquire in the books of God, the Bible and Nature, armed with human reason. The Protestant Reformation broke down old structures of authority and created new ones. Individual conscience became the basis of a new kind of civil compact, and the idea from which centuries of endeavour to establish individual civil liberty took its inspiration. The Reformation began as a movement to overcome the corruption, abuses and inaccuracies of the received religion of the Universal Roman Catholic Church. A new world, a Promised Land of faithful observance of a proper relationship to God, opened before those who made the spiritual and intellectual journey into reformed theology. Armed with their new approach to the Bible, within the fold of a reformed Body of Christ, adherents of the new denominations would build a New Jerusalem in their civic society on Earth. The Pilgrims who ventured to the New World truly saw themselves as New Israelites seeking the land of Canaan.

With high purpose, the pilgrims set out to establish a new society. 'What need we fear', wrote John Rolfe in 1617, of the 'zealous work' of establishing the Virginia colony, 'but to go up at once as a peculiar people, marked and chosen by the finger of God to possess it'.[6] As he sailed for America in 1630, John Winthrop wrote: 'We must consider that we shall be a City upon a Hill, the eyes of all people shall be upon us.'[7] Rolfe, one of the founders of the tobacco industry in the Virginia colony, and Winthrop, who became Governor of the Massachusetts colony, define the perceived purity, manifest destiny, righteousness and innocence of America. And their careers contain the contradiction that so troubles observers of America. As the Native American writer Jimmie Durham says:

Even now one may read editorials even daily about America's 'loss of innocence' at some point or other, and about some time in the past when America was truly good. That self righteousness and insistence upon innocence began as the US began with invasion and murder.[8]

For Durham, America has from the beginning had a nostalgia for itself because of actual guilt. The United States, he argues, was the first settler colony to establish itself *against*, and through the *denial* of, its original inhabitants. 'It developed thereby a narrative that was more complete, more satisfying ... That narrative has generated new cultural and political behaviour which has been a main influence in the modern world.'[9]

'The great myth' as Peter Mathiesson calls it, used to justify and sustain the seizure of America, is that what was 'discovered' was a vast wilderness. 'The New World: fresh, virginal, unaltered by human hands. And in consequence of believing in the unspoiled nature of the land found here, all culture on this continent was considered then, and is considered now by many, to have been transplanted from the "advanced" civilizations of Europe, the "Old World".'[10] The earliest settlers wrote they had found a new Eden, the land of Canaan, an earthly Paradise. Here they could begin a new experiment in society, superseding and resolving the problems, corruption, imperfections and failings of the "Old World". The freedom that the settlers appropriated for themselves is directly related to the freedom that they denied to the original inhabitants of an already peopled, settled, cultivated land, a landscape that was the product of the interaction of man and nature.

The denial that Durham refers to begins with the question of whether the native inhabitants of the New World were human beings possessed of souls at all. It runs through the conventions of the earliest descriptions of Native Americans, which are consistently negative. 'They have no ...' is the constant refrain, whether the topic is the concept of personal possessions, governance, religion, marriage. What they 'had not' was the social forms and behaviour of Europe. These negative descriptions were taken up by armchair philosophers in Europe and employed to shape a hierarchical vision of human social and cultural existence that had already been under construction when the pilgrims set foot in what became America. There is a long gestation and various phases in the 'definition by denial' of Native Americans. But what is clear is how the old and familiar reflexes of thought shaped in the medieval power rivalry between Christendom and Islam were extended to manufacture the ideas, attitudes and means of dealing with Native Americans.

Spain, the first imperial power in the New World, earnestly debated the status of the native inhabitants. The point at issue was whether Native Americans were what the Ancient Greek philosopher Aristotle had termed 'natural slaves', one part of mankind set aside by nature to be slaves in the service of those born for a life of virtue free of manual labour. It was not only the authority of the Ancients that gave this idea respectability – it also had Biblical warrant in the sons of Ham who were destined to be 'hewers of wood and drawers of water'. The first application of this idea to the New World appears in the writings of Scottish philosopher John Major, based in Paris in 1510. The idea was immediately contested. 'I am a voice crying in the wilderness' was the text of a sermon preached in 1511 by Antonio de Montesinos in a church on Hispaniola, where Columbus had made landfall. Montesinos asked: 'Are these Indians not men? Do they not have rational souls? Are you not obliged to love them as you love yourselves?' These contradictory opinions led to a series of public debates in Spain over a period of decades, resulting in a set of instructions concerning the treatment, and definition of the status, of the native peoples.

The debates were not solely a disinterested search for understanding of a new people. What Europe made of the Native Americans affected the justification and security of its claims to appropriate and possess the territory of empire. The first debate produced the Requimiento, the requirement to read out, in a language they could not understand, a formal declaration offering the Indians a choice. They could submit to Spanish rule and allow the preaching of the faith. If they refused, the Spaniards were empowered to undertake punitive measures and enter their land with fire and sword. 'We shall take you and your wives and your children, and shall make slaves of them, and as such shall sell and dispose of them as His Highness may command; and we shall take away your goods, and shall do all the harm and damage that we can, as to vassals that do not obey.'[11]

In the 1550s, when the great debates took place at Valladolid in Spain between the philosopher-theologian Juan Gines de Sepulveda (1490–1573) and the Dominican friar Bartolomé de Las Casas (1474–1566, known as 'the Apostle' to the Indians), an alternative view, and an enduring idea of empire, was put forward. Native Americans were not natural slaves. 'All mankind is one', Las Casas insisted, and went on to argue: 'And the savage peoples of the earth may be compared to uncultivated soil that readily brings forth weeds and useless thorns, but has within itself such natural virtue that by labour and cultivation it may be made to yield sound and beneficial fruits.'[12] Here is the case for Indians as 'natural children' to be taken under protection, taught, converted and brought to civilisation. The trouble with this all-embracing colonial framework is the lack of any passing-out exam. And it is rather difficult to accept the tutelage and pedagogy of one's murderers, oppressors and despoilers. The idea of the natural child was a polite fiction founded on deep racial arrogance, even when it came from a good and saintly man such as Las Casas, who wished only to expose the genocidal brutalities of his contemporaries.

The natural child philosophy lived long in European consciousness – indeed, it is with us still. It is the real text of the lecturing and hectoring offered to 'developing' nations on topics from economic policy to human rights by the developed nations that grew rich from colonialism and that still reap a windfall and unearned profit from the inequitable world economic order they built. In the 16th century, the idea of the 'natural child' was embraced by colonial rulers, not from altruism but self-interest. As persons with souls, capable of being instructed, the native inhabitants of America legally possessed sufficient competence to assign their lands, property and persons to the authority and administration of a colonial power. This resolved a vexed point of law and realpolitik. In the medieval world-view that shaped the expansion of Europe, there were four concepts that created claims to rights in newly encountered regions: conquest; agreement or cession; papal 'donation'; and original occupation (discovery). And the greatest and most secure of these was agreement or cession on the part of the inhabitants, obtained by whatever stratagem, fiction or fantasy. Slaves who were themselves property could have no property or rights to agree to cede, whereas natural children could. What was conquered could be conquered again by another European nation. Papal donation no longer had a hold over Protestant nations such as England, the Netherlands and Denmark. Original occupation was contentious – it involved obscure inquiries couched in terms of Biblical ethno-history, and was far too tenuous to apply to the New World. In the US, the treaties by which the land was appropriated – and all of the paternalist arrangements that the government made to administer the lives of the native peoples who had consigned their fate to the new republic – are called 'Federal Indian Law'. The Native American academic Vince Deloria Jr, Professor of American Indian Studies and History at the University of Colorado, has long denounced this phrase: 'It conveys almost no significant meaning, it rarely is tangent to the world of human affairs, and it covers a multitude of historical sins with the shellac of legality.'[13] The 'shellac' was manufactured from the medieval framework of legal reasoning and has been applied consistently from the outset. No matter how thick the layers, the facts beneath give the idea of justice a bad name.

The debates in Spain were avidly followed by English enthusiasts for empire. Spanish ideas and arguments passed into the repertoire of debate and informed the context in which English colonies in America were to be ventured and established. In the early English colonial literature, the whole range of Spanish responses to native peoples finds its echoes. The negative description, 'They have no ...', became the argument of 'Meum' and 'Teum'. The Indians, having no true concept of possession, no 'Mine' and 'Thine', were *users* of their land rather than owners. Therefore, by law, they could be dispossessed of the land they occupied. There were also Puritan clergy who asserted that the Indians were children of the devil who might profitably be wiped out and their lands appropriated. The approach with fire and sword was legitimated by the instructions to early colonists and honoured in their practice. Resistance was not only not tolerated, it was futile. And when no actual hostility was offered – as was the case in King Philip's War, the campaign in the Massachusetts colony (1675–6) that marked the major turning point in relations between the colonists and Indians, as Francis Jennings argues in his book, *The Invasion of America* – a little 'black ops' on the part of the settlers could manufacture an offence to justify overwhelming military response. Or the exercise of democracy could simply vote the problem of appropriating rights of ownership out of existence. In 1640, one New England assembly passed an eminently straightforward series of resolutions:

1. The Earth is the Lord's and the fullness thereof. Voted
2. The Lord may give the earth or any part of it to his chosen people. Voted
3. We are his chosen people. Voted.[14]

The debate is epitomised by John Rolfe's 'mighty war with his meditations'. Rolfe was enamoured of Pocahontas, not the recent Disney animated reformulation, but the actual woman. In a letter written in 1614, he presents his detailed arguments and search for justification in marrying Pocahontas. It reads as a forensic dissection of the justification for empire. Rolfe depicts himself and his fellow settlers as charged with the duty to make a new society, separate from the errors and corruption of Europe. To come out and be separate was a New Testament text (1 Corinthians 6:17) with a significant dual meaning in America. Pilgrims separated themselves from Europe to develop a pure and more perfect society. But this and other Biblical texts (Ezra 10:10 and Genesis 9:25) had direct import concerning marriage across ethnic and religious lines, marriage with unclean, accursed races, and therefore should be a complete bar to the marriage that he intended. Rolfe needed another line of argument to overcome what seemed an insurmountable obstacle. He found his alternative argument in the idea that Pocahontas, while clearly the daughter of an unclean, barbarous people, was nevertheless willing and able to be instructed and thus brought within the fold of Christianity, and therefore his marriage would precisely fulfil the missionary purpose of settling this New World. Pocahontas was the first and most notable convert to Christianity in what became the United States of America. It is this image, the baptism of Pocahontas, that is depicted in the Rotunda of the Capitol building. The baptism image is more important, conceptually and legally, than Captain John Smith's self-serving tall tales of Pocahontas. Smith was a soldier of fortune and one of the leaders of the first successful English colony in what became the US, who wrote a number of popular books about his experience. In only one of these did he include the story that has become the best-known myth about Pocahontas: that when Smith was about to be executed by the Powhatan Indians, the chief's daughter, Pocahontas, laid her head on his and demanded that his life be spared. Indeed, this may be the only legend of Pocahontas that most people know. It formed the centrepiece of Disney's 1995 animated film.

By the manipulation of old ideas, the New World could be brought within European conventions. The native peoples and their possessions could also be appropriated, subsumed and removed to create the actual, philosophic and legal space for the idea of America and its birth in innocence to be established. And then there was the most repugnant triumphalism of all. The pilgrim settlers soon found that native populations were dying at an alarming rate. The great pathogen invasion of new diseases – introduced by European settlers, and to which they had no natural resistance – devastated whole communities and peoples. Disease and death seemed to be opening up the country, making the land available. It was understood in the writing of the pilgrims as the Hand of Providence operating to advance the 'zealous work' of the 'chosen people'. It has been estimated that at the time of first contact there were between 20 and perhaps 50 million native inhabitants of the land that became the United States. By the 1890s, at the end of the Indian Wars and after the cataclysm of disease and the depredations of taming and settling the wilderness, the Native American population numbered 250,000.

The 'Hand of Providence' argument gave way in the 19th century to the nostalgic romance of the 'Vanishing Indian'. The passing of this 'Noble Savage', an invented abstraction, could be regretted while real people were hounded to the verge of extinction by design, by law and by political will. Both of these abstractions prefigured 'the survival of the fittest', the social-Darwinian idea of civilisations, peoples and races as being destined by nature to adapt or perish. It is not just in human law but in the making of laws of nature – in biologising social philosophy and breeding the disciplines of modern knowledge – that Western civilisation has generated 'abstractions that idealise human rationality in order to give to events and incidents a sense of meaning which they would not otherwise enjoy'.[15] Native Americans are one example, internal and instrumental to the idea of America, of a general condition that has afflicted the

Third World. In fact, their adaptation (conversion, civilising missions, development) was enforced by denial of general freedom and individual liberty, while they were pushed to extinction by acts of commission (warfare, starvation and malign neglect) and acts of omission (strategies of benign neglect, exclusion from full participation in the economy, politics and society) whose effects were as pernicious as war.

Jimmie Durham explains the process and its consequences in terms that are familiar and that echo in the experience of the peoples of the developing countries:

> The Master Narrative of the US has not (cannot be) changed. It has been broadened. It has been broadcast. This narrative is only superficially concerned with 'taming the wilderness' and 'crossing new frontiers'. The US has developed a concept and reality of the state, I might say 'statism', because US culture is so completely ideological ... The Master Narrative of the US proclaims that there were no 'Indians' in the country, simply wilderness. Then, that the 'Indians' were savages in need of the US. Then, that the 'Indians' all died, unfortunately. Then, that the Indians today are a) basically happy with the situation and b) not the real 'Indians'. Then, most importantly, that that is the complete story.[16]

The West, as much as America, has built itself as a construct of knowledge. Science and knowledge founded on reason are its special possession, and therefore it studies and knows other people better than they can know themselves. The disciplines of knowledge, such as anthropology, development studies and political science, interpret the rest of the world, not only for use in shaping the politics and policy of the West, but also in explaining the rest of the world to itself. What Durham says of Native Americans could be said of Muslims, Indians of the Subcontinent or innumerable other peoples: 'The world knows very well who we are, how we look, what we do and what we say – from the narrative of the oppressor. The knowledge is false, but it is known.'[17] For anyone who wants to understand other people, within or beyond the West, this is the most essential and awkward question to confront. 'Knowledgeable ignorance' is the familiar tradition. It is the education handed out with authority by the West to itself and to the Rest. Education, the bedrock of development programmes designed to modernise developing nations, consists in learning their history through the prism of this 'knowledgeable ignorance', and thus learning why they are inferior. It explains why battles over the content of the curriculum have been the most hotly contested part of the multiculturalism debate in the US.

Let us summarise. The ideas that made the American myth came out of Europe. They had been fashioned by European experience of its 'Hot War' with Islam and the war psychosis it produced. European identity was shaped and defined in opposition to other people, particularly Muslims, the vilified and demonised enemy. Attitudes forged over centuries on the frontier of European civilisation's fault-line with Islam were transferred to America, where they provided the motifs which made the new society possible. These old and familiar assumptions are not just history. They operate today in the unthinking reflexes, ideas and attitudes of hyper-imperialism. They are embodied in American rhetoric and policy. They are recycled in every intervention America has made in the affairs of other countries.

The truly awkward issue is not simply the recognition that invasion, murder and oppression have been done, but that institutions, values and ideas that are taken for the 'exercise of virtue' were, have been, and are responsible for the continuation of exclusion and marginalisation; and that they provide us with examples in action of the way in which 'sin grows by doing good'. In appropriating Native American land, 800 treaties were made between the various Indian nations and the United States. Some 430 were not ratified by the US Senate, though the Indians were expected, nevertheless, to abide by their provisions. As

Senator Daniel K. Inouye, a Chairman of the Senate Select Committee on Indian Affairs, observed: 'Even more tragically, of the 370 treaties that were ratified the United States proceeded to violate provisions in every one.'[18] David E. Wilkins, Native American academic and Associate Professor of American Indian Studies and Political Science at the University of Minnesota, points out that the Supreme Court is idealised as the power which prevents government action that is arbitrary, capricious, or based on prejudice. In his book *American Indian Sovereignty and the US Supreme Court: The Masking of Justice*, he studies fifteen instances in which the Supreme Court has dealt with Native American cases. 'However, the fifteen cases ... depict a Court that often acts arbitrarily, capriciously and prejudicially.' The consequences of these Supreme Court decisions

> have not only had a tremendous, often devastating, impact on tribal sovereign status and aboriginal land title but they have contributed significantly to the confusion surrounding relationships between tribal governments and the US Government. They have elevated congressional authority vis-a-vis tribal nations, and they have alternately reaffirmed and ignored the principle of judicial deference to the political branches. In addition, they have dismantled treaty rights, adversely affected the status of individual Indians, constricted – and in some cases eclipsed – tribal criminal jurisdictions, and seriously jeopardised the practise, nay, the very existence of Indian spiritual ways.[19]

If the answer to the question, 'Why do people hate America?' is 'They hate our freedoms – our freedom of religion, our freedom of speech, our freedom to vote and assemble and disagree with each other', then America has also to answer

> a larger issue of why the core democratic concepts of fairness, justice, and consent of the governed have not yet been

fully realised for tribal nations and their citizens despite clearly pronounced treaty rights, federal policies of Indian self determination and tribal self governance, positive judicial precedents, and a triple citizenship.[20]

The question of Native Americans is, as we have tried to explain, an example of a wider problem. The ideas of the natural slave or natural child have not only applied to the history of Native Americans. We have seen how Las Casas opposed the Aristotelian idea of the natural slave; nevertheless, he himself was a slave-owner. In his early career he had proposed the importing of African slaves to the Americas to spare the Indians the burden of heavy labour imposed on them. While he eventually rejected Negro slavery 'for the same reasons' as those he applied to Native Americans, as late as 1544 he owned Negro slaves. The first record of Negro slaves in North America comes in another letter written by John Rolfe, soon to be husband of Pocahontas. In 1609 he wrote that 20 Negro 'servants' were bought 'at the best and easiest rate' from a Dutch ship that put into Jamestown.[21] The growth of America, as much as the idea of America, is doubly 'contaminated by human gore',[22] and 'for the same reasons'. Slavery has made race central to the existence of America. The abolition of slavery required a bloody Civil War and the redefinition of the idea of America and its system of governance, and yet failed to eradicate the enduring marginalisation of African Americans. The 'peculiar institution' of chattel slavery was an American phenomenon, or a phenomenon of the Americas, as the eminent black academic David Brion Davis has argued: it was distinct from the form of slavery practised in the Ancient world, in medieval Europe, or in any other civilisation. It has bequeathed a peculiar and unresolved problem to America.

The multicultural debate challenges the knowledge, the disciplines of knowledge production, and the self-image fashioned out of the idea of America. It points to other facts that have not been part of the making of the idea of America. It presents the awkward question of authority over knowledge and what that means for genuine self-determination for marginalised groups. It offers not only alternative readings of history, but also alternative readings of the ideas, values and nature of other civilisations. To the simplistic call to the barricades of the 'clash of civilisations' thesis, which argues that hostility and hatred are the inevitable future that we should expect, it suggests that a different selection of unexplored facts can make a 'dialogue of civilisations' possible for those who will listen and are prepared to learn. No wonder that the multicultural debate is accused of tearing America apart and disuniting the nation.

To illustrate the way in which the multicultural debate strikes at the very heart of the American self-image, let's take as an example one awkward question: did the founders of the American nation, the authors of the Constitution, borrow and develop the concept of federal government from the example of the Six Nations Iroquois Confederation? The fate of this question speaks volumes about the freedom to disagree that exists in America. In 1977, the Native American academic, Donald A. Grinde Jr, Professor of History and Chair of the Ethnic Studies Program at the University of Vermont, published the first extensive exploration of this idea in his book *The Iroquois and the Founding of the American Nation*. Bruce Johansen, Professor of Communication and Native American Studies at the University of Nebraska, first came across the idea while interviewing Native Americans for a newspaper article marking the bicentennial of the Declaration of Independence in 1976. He made it the topic of his Ph.D dissertation, completed in 1979 and eventually, after much difficulty, published in 1982 as *Forgotten Founders: Benjamin Franklin, the Iroquois and the Rationale for the American Revolution*. Within a few years, both scholars found themselves in the midst of a fierce battle about access to, and control of, acceptable scholarly debate. They also met with passionate denunciation in the popular media as the political battle-lines on the multicultural debate were being drawn.

The point Grinde and Johansen were making was not in itself new. It already existed in literature and politics in America as an anecdote, an aside. It had been read into the Congressional Record in 1975 by Congressman William F. Walsh. In a 1960 preface to William Brandon's *American Heritage Book of Indians*, President John F. Kennedy wrote: 'The league of the Iroquois inspired Benjamin Franklin to copy it in planning the federation of States.'[23] Grinde and Johansen, however, were concerned to understand the meaning of the anecdote as history, as a different reading of Native American society, and as facts that could change the perception of the idea of America. And that is what caused all the furore.

In 1744, Benjamin Franklin was printing texts of Indian treaties, including the words of Canassatego, the chief and speaker of the Iroquois confederacy. Canassatego commended the federal system practised by the Iroquois as a model that the English colonists should adopt. In the early 1750s, Franklin observed the Iroquois Grand Council at Onondaga. The system worked as a federal republic governed by local and national councils which selected leaders by clan-based consensus. The Grand Council operated as a one-house legislature. In 1754, Franklin presented his Albany Plan for colonial union, advocating a federal system and a one-chamber legislature. Iroquois leaders were invited to Philadelphia to observe debates over the Declaration of Independence in 1775. If the history of ideas or the study of cultural diffusion have any meaning, then the bare facts provide substance for a case of influence. Iroquois influence also means that another society had, and has, ideas of individual liberty, freedom of assembly, forms of governance based on representation, and a federal structure in which democracy operates to produce peaceful negotiation of the affairs of various communities. In which case, the set of values encoded in the idea of America is simply one among various other systems based on common values that occur in different civilisations. And that is the heresy too far.

The orthodox argument holds that the ideas underpinning the Declaration of Independence and the Constitution – the specific form of the federal system of states, the states' rights, and checks and balances between the institutions that compose the political structure of America – were independent inventions based entirely on ideas derived from Europe. In particular, they were the intellectual search for the true meaning of what is called the 'Ancient Constitution', a mythic conception of individual liberties buried within the mysteries of English history. The Ancient Constitution, a chimera that also stirred the English Revolutionary era of the 1640s to the 1660s, looks back beyond Magna Carta to the Anglo-Saxons, who were, of course, invaders and dispossessors themselves, not to mention murderers, according to the Celtic peoples of the Isles of Britain. The Ancient Constitution as it exists in England is not composed only of 'black letter' law, otherwise known as written law or charters. The essence, still, of the British Constitution is that it is unwritten – that is its mystique and its great advantage. What is not written can be subtly remoulded in the hurly burly of events to permit accommodation to change. What was brought forth in Philadelphia is something different – a written constitution and a distinctive system of relations between executive, legislature and judiciary. In Philadelphia the Founding Fathers debated ideas about governance, freedom and liberty – derived from ancient society and European history – and struggled with the question of how to prevent tyranny, especially the tyranny of the passions of the populace at large. They emerged with a new answer, and that answer is pure and perfect. This orthodoxy is the basis of what writer and journalist Daniel Lazare calls American 'civic religion'. In which case, Lazare himself is a heretic, since he argues that

Society has never been more fragmented, politics have never been narrower or more short-sighted, while the extended constitutional priesthood – judges, eminent professors of constitutional law, op-ed columnists, and so forth – has never been more dogmatic. Even as they try to choke each other to death, liberals and conservatives have never been more united in their devotion to the secular religion that supposedly holds society together but is in fact tearing it apart.[24]

Constitutional faith, says Lazare, is a form of thoughtlessness: '[I]t means relying on the thought of others rather than one's own.' The Constitution, far from embodying timeless wisdom, is a time-bound answer to 18th-century problems. Taken as a distillation of ideas out of Europe that is in effect immutable, it amounts to 'a terrible dictatorship by the past over the present':

> Americans are prisoners in effect of one of the most subtle yet powerful systems of restraint in history, one in which it is possible to curse the president, hurl obscenities at Congress, and all but parade naked down Broadway, yet virtually impossible to alter the political structure in a fundamental way. They live in a system not only of limited government, but of limited democracy, which is why politics of late has become so suffocating and destructive.[25]

If the Constitution is a product of its time, then it is also a product of the experience of those who debated and framed it. If that experience included the pragmatic need to be concerned with the societies of Native Americans, then why is Iroquois influence so contentious? The condition and interactions of colonial America were more complex than the 19th-century motif of the Vanishing Indian will allow. How is it possible to establish facts about the interaction of early American and Native American societies, and yet retain a furious refusal to engage with the meaning of these facts? Pat Buchanan, right-wing politician and Presidential candidate in 2000, called the idea 'idiocy'.[26] Rush Limbaugh, the embodiment of the right in popular media, thinks that it's 'worse than historical revisionism. It's more than distortion of facts. It's the elimination of facts.'[27] Jurist Robert Bork, in his book *Slouching toward Gomorrah: Modern Liberalism and American Decline*, deemed it the work of politically motivated assassins of Western civilisation's most cherished canons.

Behind the fulminations of upholders of the Western canon stands reliance on established scholarship, the code phrase being that 'no reputable scholar' agreed with the facts about the Iroquois. In his book *Debating Democracy: Native American Legacy of Freedom* (1998), the protagonist for Iroquois influence Bruce Johansen gives a lucid and balanced history of the controversy. A recurring theme is the arrogant attitude of 'reputable' scholars, who see themselves as the gatekeepers of knowledge about Native Americans. What Johansen describes is a particular case of a familiar syndrome. The history of other societies has been fully appropriated by Western scholarship, which sees them – whether Native American, Muslim, Hindu or African – as existing in an immutable and prescriptive world of tradition. 'Tradition' is a construct that has been created by what Johansen calls 'Euro-forming' – interpreting the reality of other societies through the distorting prism of European concepts. Most essential of all, other people and their traditional ways exist in an inferior hierarchical relationship to advanced, developed, progressive Western civilisation.

The case of Iroquois influence is not only about where the Founding Fathers got their ideas. It's about the possibilities of diversity. It's about the authority, or rather lack of authority, of non-Western civilisations to represent themselves, their ideas, values and history. It's about the impossibility of an equal, respectful debate across civilisations. If this produces intolerance and fury within America, what hope is there for the rest of the world to engage peacefully and respectfully with America?

Bruce Johansen concludes his book with the thought that 'European culture is simply not imperilled by the existence of other cultures. Indeed, the peril has always flowed in precisely the opposite direction.' But self-reflection and critical questioning mean accepting a hard lesson:

> For Euro-scholars, popping the Western frame of reference into more natural proportions, as but one among many possible perspectives, may seem to diminish its stature, but that is an optical illusion. It will wear off. The truth is that Europe was never as large as its shadow made it seem.[28]

The argument about Iroquois influence challenges the conventional understanding of Native Americans, their society and history. It challenges the authority of Western scholarship. It challenges the mythic vision of where America comes from and what America means. It challenges the exclusivity and hierarchical preeminence of Western civilisation. To admit that the American Constitution was influenced by Native American ideas of democracy is to raise the spectre of America having gone hybrid. It compels the USA to face up to the last redoubt of prejudice: the disturbing prospect of intellectual miscegenation – the hybridity of its defining precepts. It is this last problem, with all its implications for identity and the definition of the American self, that stirs beneath the multicultural debate. America is a nation of immigrants, of diverse people – but everything that makes the idea of America is exclusively European, descended from a Western civilisation which is seen as superior to all the rest of the world, in spite of current American suspicion and ignorance of Europe. The point is epitomised by the neo-conservatism of the liberal historian Arthur Schlesinger Jr, in his polemical tract on the pitfalls of multiculturalism:

> Whatever the particular crimes of Europe, that continent is also the source – the unique source – of those liberating ideas of individual liberty, political democracy, equality before the law, freedom of worship, human rights, and cultural freedom

that constitute our most precious legacy and to which most of the world today aspires. These are *European* ideas, not Asian, nor African, nor Middle Eastern ideas, except by adoption.[29]

The only option that this offers the rest of the world is to submit, and keep on taking the lessons. This is ignorance on a grand scale masquerading as knowledge. The outright denial that any ideas about freedom, justice and other virtues could come from non-Western people makes dialogue with other cultures irrelevant. Such ignorant arrogance is pernicious and dangerous. It presents a two-tier world, and fuels global hatred of America. Out there, in the rest of the world, being cast into the enduring darkness of barbarism creates popular support for extreme groups whose only programme is to aggressively oppose the dominant hyperpower. To avoid a clash of civilisations, the USA must accept that all civilisations have the same right to exist, the same freedom to express themselves, and the same liberty to order their society guided by their own moral vision. Moreover, all other people of the world have the right and the freedom to disagree with America.

CHAPTER SIX

The Burden of the American Hero

In the face of fear and danger, America has drawn together, enfolded itself in national symbolism and its sustaining myths. The events of 9-11 shattered the idyll of America, the special exemption of its soil from the scourge of terrorism that besets other lands. The present reality – and future threat – of terror sent it looking for heroes. Within the conventions of American mythic narrative, that search brings to mind the moment in the classic western *Shane* (1953), when the hero who will dispense justice rides down into the green and spacious valley amid the encircling grandeur of the 'purple mountain majesties' – the cinematic expression of the patriotic song, 'America the Beautiful'.

If we want to find out why people show such animosity towards America, particularly in Western Europe, we can see part of the answer in the different reading that European audiences find in this archetypal western. What to Americans reads as an iconic vision of simple virtues made safe by a knight-errant of the wilderness, is for the rest of the world full of the ambiguity at the heart of America: violence. American political rhetoric may circle its wagons around old familiar ideas of national self-identity, with clear and certain recognition of the need for self-preservation and security. But beyond the comforting wood-smoke and firelight, outside that circle, the meaning is plain: other people will have to die. When Shane rides into the homestead of the terrorised settlers, he brings the reflexes of violence with him. Eventually he will articulate the proper response to danger, lead the defence against the onslaught of evil, and at the barrel of a gun bring the security that makes the land safe for the virtues of social progress and the fulfilment of the national mission. He will do this with ruthless brutality, dealing death to those who oppose the future course of America.

Shane is often cited as a 'coming-of-age' myth. This has less to do with the central character of little Joe, the boy who first sees the approach of Shane and quickly becomes his devotee, than with the idea of America itself. The film deals with the transition from the era of cattlemen, who replaced the trappers and woodsmen and are now to be displaced by the civilising virtues of homesteading. *Shane*, then, is a myth about rights to possession, the appropriation of just claims to righteous use of the land. Its themes are summed up in the arguments of the cattleman, Ryker: that blood is the bond that legitimates appropriation of the land. He means the spilling of blood through violence. What Shane eventually establishes is that violence is a redemptive act of justice by which civilisation is secured and advanced. *Shane* is a nostalgic elegy on how the nation, America, came to be.

The western is a mythic space in which the history, idea and themes of America are explored; and therefore an appropriate place for us to examine the notion of American self-identity and how the formation of this identity horrifies Europe. The American film theorist Richard Slotkin, Professor of English at Wesleyan University, has examined the way in which the western genre has been manipulated in succeeding phases of American history as a powerful metaphor for the nation's political communication and policy. This metaphor developed through three phases, and Slotkin examines them in considerable detail, each one clearly reflected in the titles of his books: *Regeneration Through Violence: The Mythology of the American Frontier 1600–1860*;

The Fatal Environment: The Myth of Frontier in the Age of Industrialization 1800–1890; and *Gunfighter Nation: The Myth of Frontier in Twentieth-Century America*. In each phase, he argues, violence is central to appropriation, legitimation, and the self-identity of America.

The emotive power of the mythic themes of *Shane* marks the difference between the American self-image and its narrative tradition and the outlook of the rest of the world. In the history of America, both mythic and real, individual and communal violence created the state. Unable to provide justice and security and be an effective instrument of law, the state continued to legitimate the recourse to individual and group violence to ensure the self-preservation of the people; in this way they could make the nation state a reality. The 'manifest destiny' of the mission of America was made by violence. The western, the definitive American genre, is not merely a hymn to violence – it is a view of the essential, inescapable and enduring necessity of violence to preserve civilisation. The western advances the myth that evil is intractable and can only be eradicated, that justice eventually comes down to the willingness to spill blood, that liberty resides in the right to make armed response, that the use of violence is the legitimate and only secure way to resolve a conflict. The whole world has experienced the western, and underlying its popularity is a different reaction: fear.

It may well be the hardest thing of all for Americans to appreciate how their most triumphalist national myths inspire doubt and fear in people the world over, how their most characteristic tales fuel concern and provide a rationale for why people distrust America. The fear is that the American political outlook continues to be too readily and uncritically shaped and confined by the myth of the redemptive, regenerative powers of violence. At the heart of this mythic vision stands the question: does America cherish a double standard concerning the victor and victim? In the western it is the hero – what he defends, vindicates and saves – that alone evokes poignant reflection, while the vanquished are unmourned; they do not require the reflex of regret, for as agents of evil they are by definition of less human worth. As American popular culture increasingly enfolds all stories, all histories, within its own authority and authorial power, it re-inscribes its mythic passion and moral coding onto the more complex and morally challenged ideas of the rest of the world. For the Third World, the sub-text of American story-telling is abundantly clear: they are the Red Indians, the gooks, the towel-heads and camel jockeys. What often fails to impress itself on American consciousness is that Europe, the West beyond America, is also deeply troubled, fearful and ambiguous about the sub-text of American myth.

Europe, too, has been mired in blood – both at home and in the colonial legacy abroad. But European history is the story of peoples and nations that did *not* depart to carve out a new mission statement. Its history has been formed by the internal struggle to negotiate, accommodate and incorporate the story of the vanquished within the nation as a whole, a whole that is the product of a different kind of change to that represented by the myths of America. Whether it is the story of the losers of history whose struggle has been for greater civil liberty and more equitable inclusion, or the legacy of war as the collective experience of entire populations on their native soil as well as 'over there', violence, justice, self-preservation and security create a different repertoire of responses among Europeans. Whether one is discussing advancing globalisation or building a global coalition for 'war on terror', it would be a mistake to overlook the different attitudes, ideas, and meanings that lie just underneath the surface of European collaboration with American power. Fear of the practical consequences, as well as objections to the imperatives that motivate the exercise of American power, provide a reasoned critique of why Europeans too hate America.

But to delineate the European and American attitudes to violence, it is necessary to take a closer look at the centrality of the western myth in American consciousness. America actually begins with western narratives, with fables of a frontier where the wilderness can be tamed by carrying forward the cause of civilisation. These were consciously created fables written with propagandist purpose that became the stuff of myth. All early reports of the Americas, from Columbus and Amerigo Vespucci to Captain John Smith and beyond, shared the objective of making the new world available and attractive to would-be investors and settlers. The idea of America and the themes that would become familiar in westerns were sold through popular literature to incite and secure the creation of the settler colonies. Travel literature, which included the efforts of what Percy Adams has called 'travel liars', with their obligatory adventurous exploits, was a thriving tradition that inspired the initial settlement of America and then developed to serve the making of the nation.[1]

It is easy to appreciate how readily the European tradition of Arthurian myth and legend was adapted in making the American narrative tradition. Arthurian legends were the most familiar and extensive tradition of popular vernacular literature, found in all European languages. They provided the popular setting for justifications for the Crusades against the infidel Muslims. The essence of the crusading and questing themes of Arthurian legends is the battle between good and evil, the search for purity, the vindication of civilisation through force of arms, and the understanding of adversaries as demonic. Richard Slotkin argues that another source for the origin of the western is a subtle re-ordering of the traditions of Puritan literature. Major themes in this literature, concerned with the interior struggle of Puritan consciousness, included insecurity, weakness and a sense of isolation as motive forces inspiring dependence on God, the search for surety of divine warrant for human action, and certainty of doing God's work in building the civilised life of community. Slotkin argues that the western narratives externalised these themes and found their resolution in the project of appropriating the land and taming the wilderness. The western hero embodies all of the virtues and certainties of this project, along with all of the ambiguities and the sublimated guilt that it implies. He also resolves the ambiguities of violence, an essential part of heroic response to the challenge of the wilderness.

There is no western without its hero, and the hero is always a man with a gun. In James Fenimore Cooper's novel *The Last of the Mohicans* (1826), accepted as the origin of the popular conventions of the entire western genre, the hero, Hawkeye, is a man with a very big gun who is called upon to use his knowledge of the land, his appropriation of the skills of the native inhabitants, and his mastery of the gun to open the way for, and secure the preservation of, white society. Cooper's hero was full of ambiguities, as was Cooper's own view of the advance of white settlement. But these complexities were simplified as the stuff of countless dime novels, which made their appearance in the 1860s and were busy mythologising the western frontier even as it was happening across the Mississippi. Then cinema, radio and television endlessly borrowed and reworked the conventions that Cooper had established, making the western the iconic myth of American self-identity.

Even *Shane* owes a great deal to Cooper's hero. When he rides into the valley, Shane is dressed in buckskins and wearing a gun, symbols of appropriation of the land. He, like Hawkeye before him, tries to adapt to the settled life of subduing the wilderness with hard work, until the climactic moment when he must again put on his buckskins and gun to resolve the conflict between civilisation and its adversaries by shooting the bad guys. Then, like Hawkeye, Shane rides off, leaving behind a community legitimated, regenerated, preserved and secured by violence. The quest of the homesteaders is purified by the hero's violence, the insecurities and weakness inherent in their struggle to tame the land have been resolved by it, and the dead cannot be mourned since they embodied all that was antithetical to the good and pure that was destined to triumph by its inherent worth. In short, we have all the essential elements of America's manifest destiny. Indeed, George Stevens's film is self-consciously constructed as a symbolic myth.

Ever since Cooper, the western has been central to the growth of American popular culture, a mainstay of its forms of popular entertainment, a genre that provides the location for self-reflection on America's history. It dominated the rise of cinema as a medium for assimilating and making American national identity, but not surprisingly, the western fixed American historical self-perception in a time warp. It extended, magnified and encoded a collective understanding of the meaning of the nation's ethos by embodying it in the conventions of its narrative form.

There was no getting away from the western, therefore there was no way of evading the ethic on which the western was built – and it shaped the consciousness of the American public. As John Wayne so famously put it, in his role as the Ringo Kid in *Stagecoach*: 'There are some things a man just can't walk away from.' What he meant was the violent showdown, the gun battle in which the hero legitimised the mission of America by killing whomsoever stood in his, or its, way. The heyday of the epic cinematic and television western was the era when America founded its national security state on the principle of opposition to the evil of Communism (the 'evil empire', as one-time 'B' western star, the then President Ronald Reagan, insisted it should be called), and began its career as chief Marshal in the global gun battle that this inspired. In other words, it was the era when America globalised the world-view of the western as its political outlook on international affairs; when America kept finding threats it could not walk away from in all the local bush wars and frontier conflicts across the Third World; and when it practised the doctrine that, in foreign policy, violent response was the first and only means of reliable conflict resolution.

This foreign policy, based on the western as myth and epic drama, was also the fulfilment of America's notion of manifest destiny. The idea of 'manifest destiny' was first enunciated by the polemicist John L. O'Sullivan in his political magazine *Democratic Review*. As O'Sullivan put it in his frequently quoted formulation of 1845, Americans had the right of our manifest destiny to overspread and to possess the whole of the continent which Providence has given us for the development of the great experiment of liberty and federaltive [*sic*] development of self government entrusted to us. It is the right such as that of the tree to the space of air and the earth suitable for the full expansion of its principle and destiny of growth.[2]

This continental expansion of America was merely a precursor to the full meaning of manifest destiny given by O'Sullivan in 1839, a global sense of the coming dominance of America as sole possessor of the truth and of universal human values:

[O]ur national birth was the beginning of a new history, the formation and progress of an untried political system, which separates us from the past and connects us with the future only, and so far as regards the entire development of the natural rights of man, in moral, political and national life, we may confidently assume that our country is destined to be the great nation of futurity. ... We are the nation of human progress, and who will, what can, set limits to our onward march? Providence is with us, and no earthly power can. ... For this blessed mission to the nations of the world, which are shut out from the life-giving light of truth, has America been chosen; and her high example shall smite unto death the tyranny of kings, hierarchs, and oligarchs, and carry the glad tidings of peace and goodwill where myriads now endure an existence scarcely more enviable than that of beasts of the field. Who then can doubt that our country is destined to be *the great nation* of futurity?[3]

Both elements of O'Sullivan's populist ideas of manifest destiny are comfortably accommodated in the mythic space of the western. Myth draws on the historical experience of a culture and its sources of feeling, fear and aspiration; and, as Richard Slotkin argues, it 'can be shown to function in that culture as a pre-scription for historical action and value judgement'.[4] The west-ern genre is infused with the greatest confidence in the future that is being made on the frontier, the classic locale of value judgement. Yet, the future is presented as being made by iso-lated, vulnerable and insecure outposts, constantly under threat, harassed and terrorised by agents of evil who appear in many guises but are all discernible as enemies of true civilisation. The ambiguous relationship between insecurity, the need for self-preservation, and the moral imperative of future greatness, resolves itself in the same prescription for historic action in all westerns: the hero with the gun, the man who by moral neces-sity is quicker on the draw and who eradicates the problem.

The conventions of cinematic westerns do not stay on the internal frontier of America. The western establishes the idea of freedom to roam and put down roots; and where the roots are set, that land becomes America. Like O'Sullivan's manifest des-tiny, these 'western' values go on to be universal codes that can be read into and used to structure all stories. So the struggle between good and evil elsewhere can be easily translated into the schema of a western; all stories the world over can be retold as westerns. It thus became common for Hollywood to translate 'easterns', narratives set in the East, as westerns. For example, *The Lives of the Bengal Lancers*, made in 1935, is a cavalry drama set on the North West Frontier of British India, where the enemy of civilisation is the dastardly Afghan tribesman Mohammad Khan. Not only is it easy to read Khan as an 'Indian Red Indian', the film was actually remade in 1939 as *Geronimo*, set in the American West. The convenient link between the two frontiers is the scene of a captured cavalry officer being tortured by native tribesmen, a theme that had always been a standard device of the western.

This idea of the interchangeability of frontier values was not created by Hollywood. It had been enunciated by Theodore Roosevelt, the 26th President of the United States, who in his earlier career as a writer had himself been one of the mythologisers of the American West. Roosevelt published a four-volume history, *The Making of the West* (1894–6), as well as many other books growing out of his experience of establishing a cattle ranch in the Dakota Territory in 1883. As a politician, Roosevelt was one of the architects of American Empire, the policy of expanding the idea of manifest destiny across the Pacific and around the world. Speaking of the American acquisition of the Philippines, which took place in 1898, Roosevelt declared:

> Every argument that can be made for the Filipinos could be made for the Apaches. And every word that can be said for Aguinaldo could be said for Sitting Bull. As peace, order and prosperity followed our expansion over the land of the Indians, so they'll follow us in the Philippines.[5]

True to the practice of the western, in the operation of foreign policy Roosevelt also famously observed: 'No triumph of peace can equal the armed triumph of war.'[6]

American history is, on many levels, a war narrative. The motifs and rhetoric of its internal frontier war have been externalised as a means for understanding and shaping the world. And the conventions of the cinematic western are easily read into all action genres, including war films, a point which prompted David Sterritt, film critic of the *Christian Science Monitor*, to ask:

> Could it be that Hollywood's long habit of drawing entertainment value from violence and destruction has helped shape America's immediate reaction to the Sept. 11 events – and may also influence ideas about how their country should respond to its actual and perceived enemies? The answer to the first question is probably yes.

Sterritt goes on to raise a 'more troubling' thought: '[T]hat public views of retaliation, revenge, and warfare may come more from decades of popular entertainment than from sustained reflections on history and morality.'[7] To reflect differently on history, America would first have to know the history of the rest of the world as something other than a narrative to be read according to US conventions, cultural prescriptions and value judgements. In fact, as we saw in chapter four, American popular entertainment has for decades been actively obliterating the rest of the world as a realm with a different history and recreating it in familiar American terms – the mould set by Roosevelt. Europe has a different sense of the meaning of history, and a different social philosophy growing out of this. It is the overt American tradition of rewriting history that so offends European sensibilities.

The Hollywood World War II saga *U571* is the apotheosis of a tradition of appropriating and obliterating history. *U571* deals with one of the crucial events of the war, the capture of the German Enigma code machine that eventually produced vital intelligence for the Allied cause. In the cinematic version of history, the Allied cause has been translated into an entirely American endeavour. In real history, the capture of the German submarine and its Enigma machine was carried out by British submariners in 1941, before America entered the war. In film history, it is an entirely American operation taking place in 1942. It is translated to the screen as an heroic exploit of what Richard Slotkin calls the 'good war' model.[8] War films always have a propagandist subtext, as well as being vehicles for polemics of politics and morality. For America, two World Wars, begun in and by Europe, have summoned a pacific, reluctant nation to resolve the problems of the Old World with the regenerative power of its armed involvement. American military might exercised 'over there' has been a necessary act for the preservation and security of the world. Since American economic, productive and military power was the decisive element in turning the tide of war, America was the victor. This simplified version of history distances the American outlook from that of Europe, and creates the platform for the construction of different responses to the post-war world, especially in the era of the Cold War.

America seems to have no sense of the meaning that World War I holds within European consciousness. The mass slaughter of mass-conscripted armies on the Western and Eastern Fronts fundamentally altered European society, changing the dynamics of its politics, religion, social philosophy and its view of militarism. Church attendance in Britain suffered a marked decline after World War I, the beginning of a long process. It has been traced to popular revulsion at the cynical 'God on our side' jingoism used to conscript and motivate the machine-gun fodder in a senseless, inhumane conflict. The common soldier, in the imagery of so many of the war poets, was seen as the crucified Christ sacrificed by the sin of nationalism, and the nationalist use of religion by each state as a sacrilegious and heretical obscenity. Militarism could never again have an unqualified or uncontentious place in European thought or sensibilities, which is why fascist militarism could be seen as an enemy that had to be confronted as a moral imperative in World War II.

Two world wars also gave Europe a very different popular understanding of Russia. Russia endured the same trauma of slaughter and sacrifice of the common man as the other European nations. European governments were only too afraid that their own populations would react in the same way as the Russian people. The working classes of Europe therefore read the Russian Revolution with a sympathy that did not rely on being pro-Communist or proto-Bolshevist. Socialism in Europe has always meant a great deal more than Bolshevism. World War II also gave Europeans a different perspective on Russia. The people of Europe, who directly experienced the impact on civilian populations and infrastructure caused by the devastation of modern total warfare, had profound wells of sympathy for Russia's experience of the Great Patriotic War. Europe harbours the clear understanding that, in addition to US military muscle, its 'victory' in the war against Hitler owes an enormous debt to the willingness of the Russian people to fight and die in common cause with the rest of Europe. It is a popular sentiment in Europe that this Russian contribution on the Eastern Front was probably the most decisive element in determining the course of the war.

In the post-war world, a new Cold War became America's global metaphor, its externalisation of its own western mythology as the means for understanding the whole world. And in this war, too, there was a clear difference between popular attitudes in America and in Europe. From very different historical experience, Europe had good reason to doubt, and be unmoved by, the spectre of Russian Communist power. Europe had a much more complex and instinctive understanding of the meaning of the fact that one-third of Russia's productive capacity had been destroyed in the war against Hitler. While American political rhetoric built up the Russian menace in familiar demonic terms, European popular opinion was far less credulous, both of the demonisation and of the idea that Russia had the economic capacity to take on America – let alone prevail. This proved to be the correct view. The end of the Cold War was greeted in America as a triumph of armed response, the culmination that marked the 'end of history' by global victory for the ethos of America. In Europe, the exultation owed far more to the passionate hope that a wasted half-century of Cold War hostilities and the logic of Mutually Assured Destruction (MAD), and the squandering of precious resources that it entailed, had at last ended.

When America determined that Russian Communism would be the new frontier – the civilisational divide that was found everywhere around the globe and that had to be confronted wherever it could be located – the American public had to be persuaded. If you really want all the weapons and taxes to pay for the new frontier, Senator Arthur Vandeburg advised

President Truman, then you had better 'scare the hell out of the American people'.[9] Truman proceeded to do so in a series of speeches playing up the Red Menace and citing the imminent threat to France and Italy. Both France and Italy had major Communist parties – and still do – but with their own very specific histories that owed little to Russia. Not surprisingly, the French, Italians and most Europeans found Truman's spectre of the Red Menace on the march inside Western Europe to be extremely simplistic. Indeed, the specificities of different histories colour the European understanding of all the other frontier range wars in which America justified its use of overt and covert armed response as part of its virtuous effort to contain and confront the Red Menace. There are two points of divergence between America and Europe that arise from this frontier narrative of the Red enemy.

1. America has a clear and straightforward understanding of Europe as the Old World that its people left behind. In popular imagination and imagery, they left it stalled in the corruption and decay that they were so anxious to flee. To borrow the language of O'Sullivan, if the problem of European history had been 'the tyranny of kings, hierarchs, and oligarchs', which in rich measure it had been, then America seems to have little sense that Europe has wrestled these demons into an acceptable form of submission by its own means and on its own terms. The politics and society of Europe are as flawed, but not worse than that of America, and Europe reserves the right to think that it has at least as much moral conscience, devotion to freedom, human rights and civic virtue, as America. When central casting of fiendish villains in contemporary Hollywood films requires an obligatory European actor, Europe has cause to seriously question whether America really acknowledges any parity between the two cultures. European nations have their own history of racism, colonialism and decolonisation; they have been resisted and fought out of their colonies and then had to sit

down and negotiate with, and accept as partners, many whom they have previously called terrorists and portrayed as demonic enemies – such as Jomo Kenyatta, leader of the Mau Mau insurgents, who became the first Prime Minister of an independent Kenya, and Nelson Mandela himself, now a secular saint, who was dubbed a terrorist by Margaret Thatcher. It has been a salutary lesson that has shaped a distinct European political outlook on global affairs.

2. European experience of two world wars did not find violence redemptive, and the very idea of a Third World War was quite repugnant to European popular opinion – that's why CND (the Campaign for Nuclear Disarmament) and the peace movement in general had such deep roots in Europe. The western genre could not create the same psychic space in Europe. In America, the western was the perfect mythic space for scaring the hell out of the citizens. The birth of the Cold War coincided with the peak of popular exposure to the western in America through cinema, radio and the new invention of television. So we arrive back in the valley with the simple, vulnerable homesteaders in *Shane*, anxious to secure their future through individualism and hard work. The coming-of-age experience for young Americans in the early 1950s, when *Shane* was released, included regular drills hiding under their school desks to save themselves from nuclear fallout deposited by Russian warheads: paranoia and insecurity as the basis of normal life, just like the homesteaders who expected daily terrorism from the cattlemen. In *Shane*, the other aspect of the coming-of-age myth is personified by the young boy, little Joe, the proto-America. The deeply troubling fact is that this youngster is presented as eager for violence, constantly impressed by violence, fascinated by weaponry, anxious to learn how to use the gun. It is little Joe who runs after Shane to witness the final shootout, and who provides the most poignant and memorable of film endings, plaintively calling to Shane to come back as he rides off into the great beyond. What

does he say as his voice resounds to the echo? 'Pa's got things for you to do, and Mother wants you. I know she does. Shane. Shane! Come back! Bye, Shane.' The lost hero has provided redemption, security and the preservation of the fledgling community through violence. He is longed for and desired. This is not a final goodbye: such heroes and such tactics will be needed again. Indeed, Shane returns in the movies as Clint Eastwood's 'man with no name', notably in *Pale Rider* (1985).

If recourse to violence is an original and necessary part of the rhetoric of America, then it is hardly surprising to find violence reified to a form of communication. Lewis Lapham, Editor of *Harper's Magazine*, notes that in the summer of 1965 the then US Secretary of State for Defense, Robert McNamara

> defined the bombing raids that eventually murdered upwards of two million people north of Saigon as a means of communication. Bombs became metaphors meant to win the North Vietnamese to a recognition of America's inevitable victory, and American planes dropped what came to be known as 'bomb-o-grams' on civilian as well as military targets, less for tactical than for rhetorical reasons. By no means unique in his suppositions, McNamara was both the product and the servant of a society that likes to express itself in the grammar of violence, and he was caught up in a dream of power that substituted the databases of a preferred fiction for the texts of common fact. What was real was the image of war that appeared on the flowcharts and computer screens. What was not real was the presence of pain, suffering, mutilation and death.[10]

It is this American propensity to eulogise violence and not to contemplate its human cost, not to empathise with the human experience of the consequences of violence, that strikes fear and enmity into the hearts of people the world over. The rest of the world may not know the origins of this violence, but Europeans know both its origins in American history and its location in American consciousness. In westerns the hero may be hurt, but he rallies to save the day, and the enemy is dispatched with purely positive consequences. The Vietnam War familiarised the whole world with the chilling and despicable phrase 'collateral damage'. Those collaterally exterminated, it appears, count as less than real people. It is not that innocents have never died in European wars – they always do; it is American unwillingness to reflect on, or even use honest language to describe, ruined lives that makes people believe that America's freedom to enjoy life, liberty and the pursuit of happiness is the only exercise of these prerogatives that matters.

The use of violence abroad in order to make the world safe and compliant to the American way has been the history of the last half of the 20th century, as we saw in chapter three. That this stimulates endless protest and a firm conviction of secondary status among people of the Third World is one agenda that America resolutely chooses to ignore. That it raises just as much doubt, rage and fear in Europe seldom makes it onto the radar of American political consideration. When Ronald Reagan decided to send a warning bomb-o-gram to Libya in 1986, using US bases in Europe as a terrestrial aircraft carrier, it was not only European public opinion that was incensed. Politicians openly voiced their fear that NATO was being manipulated to the point of fracture. American opposition to the proposed European rapid reaction force seems perverse in the face of constant American complaint that it is shouldering the burden of defending freedom alone and at its own cost; and it fails to engage with the serious political debate about the increasing distance between the American view of the world and that of European nations. All this promotes the strong conviction that America is a nation that has lost – if it ever had – the capacity to respond to any challenge, crisis, dispute or difference of opinion by negotiation, accommodation or serious dialogue.

The reasons for this inability, argues Lewis Lapham, are to be found within America itself. In an essay on the terrorist bombing of the Alfred Murragh Building in Oklahoma City in 1995, Lapham asks: 'How do we construe the American idea of freedom if we must communicate with one another by bomb-o-gram?'[11] The most awful implication of the Oklahoma bomb was that it was designed, as many commentators noted, to be understood in the tradition of regenerative violence. In a letter to a newspaper in 1992, Timothy McVeigh, the bomber, had asked: 'Is Civil War imminent? Do we have to shed blood to reform the current system?' In answer to his own question, Lapham states that McVeigh turned '4,800 pounds of fuel oil and ammonium nitrate into a press release'.[12] Indeed, in America the use of violence to make an emphatic statement is a well established tradition. As a commentator noted in *The New Yorker*:

> [The Oklahoma] bombers ... fit all too well into that bloody tradition, and are all too faithful to its code: Stop thinking of the other person as a person and start thinking of him as an occasion – a blank slate on which to inscribe the Thought for the Day.[13]

America is not only a nation in which random violence is an everyday occurrence; in which the possibility of being shot by a mugger for the sake of a few dollars or a wristwatch is a routine fear of any citizen; in which drive-by shootings and armed road rage are common. It is also a country in which disaffected teenagers take their guns to school and shoot people, a place where mass slaughter has become a commonplace for the depressed, disaffected and disturbed. The rhetoric of violence has become an integral part of the American political scene. As the US has become a polarised nation of two cultures, liberal and conservative, unable to communicate by political debate since the differences occur within the narrow spectrum of

Republican and Democrat, it has become a country in which the politics of the bomb-o-gram has established itself. So some of those who passionately defend the right to life of an unborn foetus can bomb an abortion clinic and assassinate doctors who perform abortions. For Lapham, it is indicative of the true dimensions of America's contemporary problem:

> The commonwealth of shared meaning divides into remote worlds of our own invention, receding from one another literally at the speed of light. We need never see or talk to anybody with whom we don't agree, and we can constitute ourselves as our own governments in perpetually virtuous exile. For every benign us, we can nominate a malignant them ...; and for every distant they, a blessed and neighbouring we.[14]

If America has become a country that cannot debate, engage or negotiate with itself, cannot wrestle with different meanings among people who are all Americans, then what hope is there that it can extend a listening ear or open mind to the rest of the world? This is what troubles most people in Europe about America. And this is what leads many Europeans, particularly those who lean towards the left, to denounce America in such harsh and uncompromising terms.

Before 9-11 there were many commentators reading the signs of decay, corruption and decadence in the political culture of America. The inability of finding any political resolution to the issue of violence was a prime example of the more general malaise. It is incomprehensible to Europeans, for example, how a late 18th-century pronouncement about the right to bear arms can be a conundrum incapable of political resolution at the beginning of the 21st century, in a nation daily beset by bloodletting at the point of a gun. America is regularly shaken, but not stirred to any remedial legislative action on the question of gun control, thanks to the competing pressures of its own irreconcilable ideas. In Europe, an armed citizenry has never been an acceptable idea to tyrant kings, hierarchs or oligarchs, any more than it has to dedicated democrats. Access to guns is strictly controlled, and the infection of armed criminal violence exported by American popular culture is profoundly feared. When a mass shooting occurred in Britain in 1996 at Dunblane, where a lone gunman opened fire in a primary school, legislation was immediately introduced and speedily enacted to further restrict access to guns, with the overwhelming support of the population. In Europe, the gun has no mystique; it is generally understood to be a dangerous offensive weapon and treated as such. European countries have known and lived with political terrorism at home for some time, as we noted in chapter one. The terrorists have been resolutely opposed by governments, and yet it has always been part of the European belief that ultimately, even with the help of America as a third-party mediator, political resolution of grievances rather than wholesale extermination would be the necessary outcome. In culture and politics, Europe stands wondering at the reflexes that motivate America.

Since 9-11, the internal state of American society and culture and the intractable issues they raise have, far from being resolved, been submerged by patriotic outpourings and the constraints that this has placed on public and political debate. With enormous sympathy and sadness, European nations shared the trauma of 11 September with America. But the way in which America has responded – and will continue to respond – to those attacks, is a source of genuine fear among Europeans. American anguish and demand for armed response has operated according to the logic of American myth. In an article for *The Chronicle of Higher Education*, Richard Slotkin noted how America used the conventional myths of the western to mobilise its response:

> So far I see two myths being deployed. ... One is the myth of 'savage war' based on the oldest US myth, the myth of the frontier. The myth represents American history as an Indian war, in which white Christian civilization is opposed by a

'savage' racial enemy: an enemy whose hostility to civilization is part of its nature or fundamental character, an enemy who is not just opposed to our interests but to 'civilization itself' ...

The other myth we have invoked is the myth of the 'good war', summoned by the invocation of Pearl Harbor.

The danger in our present use of myth is that our myths of choice may be so at odds with reality that their imperatives can never be fulfilled ... Total victory may not be possible. To invoke the 'good war' myth is to raise expectations that cannot be fulfilled, and failure will discredit both the myth itself, and the administration that invokes it (as happened in the Vietnam War).

If events do not follow the course prescribed in our 'good war' myth, we may revert to the 'savage war' scenario – and this is a dangerous myth. It expresses, and also empowers, the profound sense of rage we feel when we have helplessly suffered a terrible trauma, and it rationalizes a limitless, ruthless, and perhaps irrational use of force against those nations and peoples associated with our enemies.[15]

American myths, the ethos of the western, provide US foreign policy with a broad licence for extraordinary violence and the rhetoric of the bomb-o-gram. But they also legitimate, and remind America of, its deep sense of aloneness, of being distinct from the rest of the world. If even Europe, culturally so close to America, its partner in Western civilisation and the supposed ancestral source of the ideas that define America, can neither debate with, caution nor counsel America in its determination to answer terrorism by recourse to its mythic agenda, then it is no surprise if reasonable fear of the capabilities and sensibilities of the sole hyperpower should move beyond fear and begin to crystallise into hatred. The proposition that there is something hateful in the very nature of America, that its myths present life-threatening danger to the rest of the world, appears quite natural.

CHAPTER SEVEN

Hating America and Transcending Hatred

In Mathieu Kassovitz's film *La Haine* ('Hate', 1995), three young men living in a Parisian housing project discover the meaning of hatred. This multicultural group – Vinz, moody and intense, Jewish and working-class; the fun-loving Arab, Said; and Hubert, an introspective black African boxer – has little to do but kill time, their alienation consolidating a real sense of kinship. These adolescents have no jobs, no money and, even more important, no prospects of any kind. So, they hang out much like any inner-city group of marginalised young men, drifting aimlessly through the streets and suburbs. But doing nothing has its consequences, particularly when the police have singled you out as a possible source of criminal activity.

Kassovitz, who won the directorial prize at Cannes, is concerned with showing that marginalisation itself is a form of violence; that it leads to other types of violence, feeds back on itself and eventually spirals out of control. The film's protagonists are not particularly bad or violent individuals. They are simply humans trying to be human, with all their strengths and faults. But their ethnicity and appearance, their class and social backgrounds, have labelled them as inferior and violent. So that's the way they are treated by society in general, and by the police –

who do not hesitate to torture the boys – in particular. And, in their turn, the boys' hatred is a compound product of their economic marginalisation, their cultural and racial treatment, and their own interpretation of their existence.

While the world out there may not condone their behaviour, it would certainly sympathise with the plight of the gang in *La Haine*. For much of the developing world, too, has been ruthlessly marginalised and culturally abused. The fictional characters of *La Haine* largely direct their hatred towards the police, who are both the immediate cause of their suffering and the representatives of an authoritarian establishment. The real world directs its resentment towards America, the global hyperpower that behaves much like the police in *La Haine*; an empire unlike any in history, that has systematically rubbed everyone else's nose in the dirt.

However, no one actually *wants* to hate American people. Who would want to hate Denzel Washington or Sydney Poitier, Halle Berry or Whoopi Goldberg, Muhammad Ali or Tiger Woods, John Steinbeck or Arthur Miller, Gore Vidal or Susan Sontag? What most people hate is 'America', the political entity based on authoritarian violence, double standards, self-obsessed self-interest, and an ahistorical naivety that equates the Self with the World. Indeed, there are many obvious reasons to hate America. Three of the most commonly cited are: American support for Israel, which is seen by many in the Arab world as a US-armed and -funded colony; Washington's support for authoritarian regimes such as those in Egypt, Saudi Arabia and Algeria; and the all-too-frequent American military interventions in the developing world. But these reasons are simply that: obvious. Moreover, many other frequently cited reasons for hating America often come wrapped in equal amounts of love. For example, American popular culture, ranging from Hollywood films to pop music, inspires both love and hate in equal measure, as if the two passions were inseparable parts of a single whole. So America often seduces and horrifies at the same time.

To appreciate the scope and extent of the hatred, we need to go beyond the obvious. This is what we have tried to do in this book. We also need to be aware that dislike for America is not confined to certain groups such as Muslims, or 'fundamentalists', or European left-wing intellectuals. There are hardly any universals left in our postmodern times, but loathing for America is about as close as we can get to a universal sentiment: it is the one dynamic that unites fundamentalists and liberals, Arabs and Latin Americans, Asians and Europeans, and even the over-shadowed Canadians, with the rest of the world. Such a universal phenomenon must have a truly subterranean rationale.

The action in *La Haine* takes place in an unforgiving environment. Kassovitz sets his film in concrete suburbs that exude inhumanity. These empty vistas not only parade their hostility to the three young men, they make it impossible for them to breathe, to exist, to prosper as human beings – to be themselves. American governments and corporations have, over a period of decades, created a similarly bleak global context, a world that makes life difficult, and sometimes impossible, for many cultures and societies. Hatred for America thus has a deeper mooring; it is located in the imposed inability of other societies and cultures to exist as full and free entities, to live as they would wish to live. This confinement of cultures is not limited to the domain of politics – it extends into a wider conceptual sphere; and it is here that the four main reasons for objecting to the USA are to be found.

1. The first reason is existential. The US has simply made it too difficult for other people to exist. In economic terms, this is a stark reality for the majority of the world's population. As we have seen, the US has structured the global economy to perpetually enrich itself and reduce non-Western societies to abject poverty. 'Free markets' is simply a euphemism for free mobility of American capital, unrestrained expansion of American corporations, and free (uni-directional) movement of goods and

services from America to the rest of the world. The US dollar is the world's main reserve currency, the medium that everyone needs to pay for their foreign imports, and there is no restraint on the US's ability to print its own currency to finance its trade deficits with the rest of the world. Since international lending is carried out in dollars, crisis-ridden borrowing countries saddled with trade deficits always have to take on dollar debt burdens greater than their capacity to repay. Couple this with the US control of international financial institutions such as the IMF, World Bank and WTO, and we see how the world economy functions to marginalise the less-developed world. We are moving towards a world in which global markets in such basic things as healthcare, welfare, pensions, education and food and water are supplied and controlled by American corporations. The ability of developing countries to provide universal access to basic social services has been systematically and ruthlessly eroded. This is why absolute poverty has increased over the past decades; and the gulf between the rich and poor has now reached unimagined depths. America is literally taking bread out of the mouths of the people of the developing world.

Politically, two simultaneous processes are reducing the choices and freedoms of the rest of the world. The process of *enlargement*, the expansion of the reach and influence of America – through trans-national economic regimes and multinational capital as well as aggregation of power from supposedly multi-lateral institutions such as the World Bank, IMF and WTO to the United States – is simultaneously, in effect, a process of hier-archical *integration* of the rest of the world. The world is being integrated in the shape of a rigid, iron-clad pyramid. Those at the bottom of the pyramid are not just economically excluded, they are also politically contained. So their political existence is as perilous as their economic reality.

Moreover, American-led globalisation has also shrunk cultural space. Even the most economically and politically disadvantaged people seek cultural expression and fulfilment. But the pyramid-shaped globe allows little room for other cultures to exist as such, let alone permit the full expression and flowering of non-Western cultures. Quite simply, there is no space left for difference to exist on its own terms and within its own categories.

Thus, existence *per se* – physical, political and cultural – has become a problem for the developing world. Like the protagonists of *La Haine*, the people of the Third World are angry at their existential condition. They see America as the main culprit and the continuing source of their predicament; and thus direct their hostility towards it.

2. The second major reason for objecting to America is cosmological. In the conventional cosmological argument for God, derived originally from Aristotle, God is described as the cause of everything; this is why some versions of this argument are called the 'first cause' argument. In today's globalised world, America is seen as the prime cause of everything. Nothing seems to move without America's consent; nothing can be solved without America's involvement. Only America can resolve the conflict between Palestine and Israel; only America's intervention can lead to some sort of resolution between India and Pakistan over Kashmir; and it was America's involvement in Northern Ireland that brokered a political settlement. Without American ratification, the Kyoto Treaty on carbon dioxide emissions is not worth the paper it is written on; without an American nod, nothing moves at the WTO or World Bank; and without America, the UN ceases to be a United Nations. At the global level, America is both the first cause and the sustaining cause.

The cosmological grounds for resentment also relate to the 'gigantism' of America itself. A Chinese proverb says that the tallest tree attracts the most dangerous winds during a typhoon. As a tree with branches that touch every corner of the globe, America is a natural target. But this is compounded by the hubris that is an integral part of the cosmological structure that America cannot see. Western empires – Roman, Spanish, British

– were concerned with sustaining and enhancing their control of subject populations. America has taken this principle to a new quantum level: American empire is a colonisation of the future that becomes a total consumption of all space and time – rewriting history, changing the very stuff of life in our genetic structure, shifting weather patterns, colonising outer space, indeed, changing the course of evolution itself! It is this height and breadth of arrogance that startles and, not surprisingly, terrifies most of the world. If there are no limits, what is there to stop the US from actually consuming the non-American people of the world? Inducted in the cosmological structure of America, the rest of the world will vanish. While travelling on the metro, the three teenagers of *La Haine* see an advertising billboard with the bold caption: 'The World is Yours.' They delete the 'Y', making the point that 'the world' does not include all of us. It seems to belong only to those with limitless possibilities, those who have restructured the world to their own cosmological outlook.

3. The third main reason for anti-American feeling is ontological – that is, relating to the very nature of being. Once again, this takes us back to standard arguments for God. The ontological argument for God's existence, attributed to St Anselm, goes something like this: God is the most perfect being; it is more perfect to exist than not to exist; therefore, God exists. It is, of course, a circular argument. Ontological arguments infer that something exists because certain concepts are related in certain ways. Good and evil are related as opposites. So, if evil exists, there must also be good. America relates to the world through such circular, ontological logic: because 'terrorists' are evil, America is good and virtuous; the 'Axis of Evil' implicitly positions the US and its allies as the 'Axis of Good'. But this is not simply a binary opposition: the ontological element, the nature of American being, makes America *only* good and virtuous. It is a small step then to assume that you are chosen both by God and history. How often have we heard American leaders proclaim

that God is with them; or that history has called on America to act?

But appropriating goodness to one's self, and then doing evil, spells hypocrisy to others. Bruce Tonn, Professor in the Department of Urban and Regional Planning at the University of Tennessee, Knoxville, notes: 'People around the world constantly ask why the US says one thing and does something totally opposite; why the standards it wants to impose on others do not apply to the US itself. How can the United States claim to be the repository of Goodness yet have such disdain for the poor and deny them the basic right to food and water? People dying of AIDS in sub-Saharan Africa wonder why Americans can afford super computers and stealth bombers but cannot help them afford AZT and other drugs. People living in and around tropical rainforests cannot understand American criticism of their management of these crucial resources while Americans continue to trash their own environment, from destroying their wetlands to increasing emissions of global warming gases such as carbon dioxide. Europeans cannot fathom why the United States does not support global environmental protection, land mine treaties, or strong provisions to control biological and nuclear weapons or why the United States insists on selling Europeans meat and grains that are tainted with steroids and the result of genetic engineering. Russians and East Europeans do not understand why America insists on imposing economic measures on their countries that increase inequality by every criteria known to humanity. Canadians rue the impact of American culture on their own society.'[1]

Then there are the hypocritical elements of American society itself. The O. J. Simpson trial highlighted the institutionalised lying that forms the basis of American trial law for the entire world to see. The trial also brought to the world's attention the anger that many American people of colour harbour toward their government, and their deep scepticism about the fairness of the US legal system. The Clinton impeachment trial demonstrated the hypocrisy of the political establishment: conservative politicians, many of whom were also guilty of sexual 'misconduct', had no qualms in their attempt at political assassination. The Florida election debacle highlighted America's hypocrisy concerning democracy: not counting everyone's vote is only an egregious sin if it occurs in fledgling democracies of the developing world. All the people of the world duly noted that the US Supreme Court decided the outcome of the election by finding reasons not to recount all of the votes.

Why, people around the world keep asking, is the American public, in a country with the world's most advanced education system and institutions of learning, so exceedingly ignorant of world affairs? They don't know the names of the leaders of other countries, even those of their allies in the West. They don't know where other countries are located. They don't know the history of the world. They apparently don't care, either. They care about their cars, their second homes, about not paying taxes, about low gasoline prices. But why don't they care about the rest of the world? Why do Americans tend towards an insidious distrust of others, and show such neglect for the needs, desires and hopes of the rest of the world? Why?

Of course, neither America, the political entity, nor many Americans, can hear these questions. The USA may be an open society, but it's also a closed circle. Outside concerns and voices cannot penetrate the impregnable ontological walls of America. What could others – ontologically removed from being good – possibly have to tell the good, innocent and virtuous people chosen by God and history? And if America does think of them at all, what other formula can there be than the self-evident dictum that what's good for America must necessarily be good for everyone? It's not surprising that Americans are perpetually wrapping themselves in the flag, the symbol of their ontological goodness. Since the flag represents everything that is good, it must, in American eyes, attract reverence from all quarters. But to the rest of the world it's just a piece of cloth, wrapped around delusionary ideas of innocence and goodness, and shrink-wrapped in the cling-film of American corporate capitalism. The US media projects American hypocrisies on a global scale, a formula for a vicious circle of hatred. Hatred breeds hatred: ontological presumptions of goodness foster ontologically grounded hatred, which leads to its own inevitable conclusion.

4. The fourth major reason for hostility towards America has to do with definitions. America is not just the lone hyperpower – it has become the *defining* power of the world. America defines what is democracy, justice, freedom; what are human rights and what is multiculturalism; who is a 'fundamentalist', a 'terrorist', or simply 'evil'. In short, what it means to be human. The rest of the world, including Europe, must simply accept these definitions and follow the American lead (which, in most cases, Britain does exceptionally faithfully). But America defines all these things in singular terms – in terms of American self-identity, history, experience and culture, and, more often then not, in terms of American self-interest. So when President Bush, for example, says in his 2002 State of the Union address, 'America will lead by defending liberty and justice because they are right and true and unchanging for all people everywhere', he takes it for granted that American ideas of liberty and justice are the only ones that there are. There is no scope for these values to be interpreted and practised in different ways; no sense that the history and experience of other cultures may have generated their own notions of freedom and justice.

We can see this most clearly in terms of human rights issues. The Western, liberal notion of human rights equates it solely with individual political and civil freedoms. The US has reduced it further and redefined it in terms of market forces and 'free trade'. Despite enormous efforts by developing countries for over two decades, the US refuses to acknowledge that the right to food, housing, basic sanitation and the preservation of one's own identity and culture are far more important than the preservation of market forces. The UN Social Development Summit, held in March 1995, was an attempt to incorporate these concerns and reshape the human rights agenda. But, as in all such attempts, 'global market forces' won the day at the insistence of the US. As the Malaysian political scientist and human rights activist Chandra Muzaffar notes, 'of what use is the human rights struggle to the poverty-stricken billions of the South if it does not liberate them from hunger, from homelessness, from ignorance, from disease?'[2]

But the American definition of human rights is not immutable; it is a moveable feast. Thus, while the US considers the struggle of the Muslims in East Turkestan against China as a 'human rights issue', it rejects the proposition that the struggle of Chechen Muslims against Russia has anything to do with human rights. Muslims happen to be in the majority in both Chechnya and East Turkestan, and are fighting for independence in both places. On the whole, the US has ignored human rights violation in China, because China is a trading partner of increasing importance. But when US intellectual property rights were at risk, human rights came quickly to the fore, and even a trade war was threatened to induce Chinese cooperation. It is because of their narrow definition and shifting nature that US ideas of 'human rights' are frequently described by thinkers of developing countries as the most evolved form of American hyper-imperialism. The US defines human rights as it wishes, then uses the emotive language of human rights as a stick to beat any country that does not fall in line with its economic policies.

The much-vaunted universal precept of 'freedom of the press' gets similar treatment. When it comes to other countries, it is defined as a universal imperative. When freedom of the press ends up with criticism of America, it becomes dangerously subversive. So the US went out of its way to stop Qatar-based Al-Jazeerah, the only independent satellite television station in the Arab world, from broadcasting from Afghanistan. It placed enormous pressure on Qatar to 'rein in' Al-Jazeerah, and eventually bombed its office in Kabul. Early in 2002, the US closed down the Palestinian independent weekly *Hebron Times*. The Palestinian Authority let it be known that 'CIA officials had recommended the closure of the paper for being overly critical of Israel and US policy towards the Palestinian people'.[3] The editor of the *Hebron Times*, Walid Amayreh, declared: 'It is lamentable that the United States which values press freedom at home is bullying the Palestinian Authority to suppress freedom in Palestine. What happened to the American First Amendment, or maybe it doesn't apply to non-Americans?'[4]

The uniquely self-interested way in which America defines and redefines human rights, and then uses them as an instrument of its foreign policy, sends a dual message to the world. It suggests that, on the one hand, abiding by the constraints imposed by human rights is mainly for others, not for America; while on the other hand, it delivers a clear message to developing countries: adopt economic policies recommended by America, even at the expense of human rights. Not surprisingly, this approach generates a great deal of hatred for the US.

The power to define also extends to representation: America defines the way in which other people should be seen and characterised. The US is the storyteller to the world. For the most part, the stories it tells are either based on its own experiences or, if appropriated from other cultures, given a specifically American context. This power to define others in terms of American perceptions and interests often leads to the demonisation of entire groups of people. Consider the way in which all Arabs are seen as 'fundamentalists', all those who question the control of science by American corporations as anti-science, or those who question American foreign policy as 'morally bankrupt', 'nihilists' or 'idiots', as we saw in chapter one.

The US operates its foreign policy and relates to the rest of the world on the basis of the four conceptual categories discussed above. They have become axiomatic for America: they are as integral to American self-identity as the 'self-evident truths' – such as 'all men are created equal' – that the Founding Fathers spoke about (but which they also provided Constitutional warrant to deny in practice). Inasmuch as human beings think with concepts, and move within paradigmatic beliefs, these categories have become as natural to America as breathing. This is why Americans are happy to consume most of the resources of the world, insist on exceptionally cheap petrol, and expect to be provided with an endless variety of cheap, processed food – because America is the cosmos. Just as all stories, all human experiences, are the precursor to the establishment of the US, so all futures are essentially the future of the United States. In the final analysis, America regards the rest of the world as it perceived the Red Indians – as 'natural children' that can be taught and brought to civilisation according to the demands of that American future.

Not surprisingly, the rest of the world begs to differ. Different societies find different objections within the four conceptual categories. For example, existential reasons play an important part in Africa and the poorer parts of Asia and Latin America. Cosmological reasons have generated an intense loathing for America in Europe, particularly in environmental and left-wing circles. Ontological reasons are responsible for anti-American feeling in the Muslim world, as well as in Europe. The power of America to define key notions has generated enormous resentment in China and India and among Muslim people in general. Collectively, the four conceptual planes ensure that enmity towards America is almost as universal as the desire for fresh, unpolluted air.

Clearly, it is not in the world's best interests for this hatred to continue. But can there be transcendence? Hatred, as we have already argued, is a body of opinion and ideas with an emotional baggage of prejudice that operates in an ongoing relationship, as part of a context of interaction. But hatred always simplifies. So from the point of view of the less-developed world, we have America, the Great Satan, the hyperpower, the motive factor in all that is wrong, that everywhere prevents sensible and responsible self-determination and humane solutions. And we have, from the American point of view, the only answers to the human future: freedom, democracy, liberty, free speech and free market forces, all under attack from evil enemies who are beyond moral persuasion and therefore must be rooted out and killed for the preservation of the good, which is endlessly vulnerable to attack because of its openness and honesty. This is a cartoon version of reality on both sides. But in a world dominated by sound-bites and short attention spans, and tightly controlled media, the cartoon version goes from strength to strength because it looks like a believable, gripping narrative that explains everything. The antidote is to learn to love complexity and refuse to be frightened by stories of bogeymen and monsters under the bed. We have, as a wise man once said, 'nothing to fear but fear itself'. The entire purpose of simplified narratives is to make us, and keep us, afraid of the great big complex world out there.

Hatred makes monolithic monsters of people whose differences include common values, similar aspirations and human feelings. Transcending stereotypes can begin by unpicking one of the most precious of human ideals – that all men and women are created equal – and understanding it in a more complex way. That all are created equal is both a 'self evident' truth and meaningless if it remains 'self evident' rather than explored, questioned and permitted to express difference and diversity. All people are indeed created equal, but live with the actual inheritance of human inequalities, the legacy of real history. Equality of opportunity, equal right to exercise the liberty to be themselves, equal freedom to define and live out their beliefs as they understand them, requires more than just treating everyone the same. The libertarian rhetoric of equal rights and self-evident equal creation can be as doctrinaire, illiberal, intolerant and inequitable as any ideological system. A world in which people are created equal can be a world of difference, where diversity too has its rights. To do justly and fairly by everyone, to be genuinely equitable to all, it is necessary to be adaptable and to see the same ideal, the same end, achieved through different means in different places. This would be a world that could not be paraphrased in a sound-bite, a world dependent upon the responsibility to learn more about each other, and most of all a world prepared to accept the necessity to defer to other peoples' judgements.

Hatred works through insecurity and paranoia. It creates a political discourse of self-defensive, pre-emptive, aggressive posturing. Where insecurity and paranoia rule, we invite the dialogue of the deaf, negotiation and consultation by mutual harangues, name-calling, vilification and blame. Hatred generates parallel universes of self-justification and the ethos of the bomb-o-gram. Insecurity and paranoia make the first strike the first resort of choice in a political arena that has all the sophistication of a children's playground ruled by the ethics of the bully. Where in such a world is there any hope of transcendence? The culture of violence, the political rhetoric of the bomb-o-gram, has to be opposed everywhere. But it will be opposed only when there is genuine commitment to alternative means of communication. Political arenas and institutions have to become effective and responsive in offering negotiation, accommodation and the capacity to act.

The antithesis of hatred is trust and confidence. The problem at present is that the rest of the world has no trust in America, no confidence in American willingness or ability to use its immense power responsibly, or indeed to define the use of its power for anything except selfish motives, to recognise the common good as anything other than its own self-interest. As the hyperpower that straddles the world militarily, politically, economically and culturally, America is a real presence in the life of all nations of the world. Its wealth and abundance are derived from its relations with the rest of the world. America cannot, therefore, pick and choose about being engaged or disengaged from the consequences of the global system that sustains its lifestyle. 'No taxation without representation', said the discontented gentlemen of the English colonies who began the American Revolution. The rest of the world, with good reason, might say the same. The more America acts like King George's England in its relations with the rest of the world, the more it legitimates revolutionary malcontents, a world that wishes to secede from America.

Hatred is sustained by wilful, 'knowledgeable ignorance'. Transcending hatred and its perverse expressions is a work of knowledge, of rethinking the limitations of what we have learnt and what we think we know. For centuries, Muslims, Indians, Chinese and many others have been told that theirs are traditional civilisations, stultifying, atrophied and rendered incapable by their traditional world-views. In truth, the West too, and America in particular, has become a traditional civilisation, with all the rigidity and sanctimonious sense of its inherent rightness that it has been so ready to condemn in other civilisations. The challenge for everyone is to make the transition from dead traditionalism – the substitution of the opinions of dead good men for doing one's own thinking – to living tradition, using cherished values and concepts as systems of critical questioning and adaptive devices to create meaningful change. The debates and ideas about revitalising tradition in the non-West are usually invisible and inaudible, but they have a great deal to teach the West. Dead traditionalism closes minds, fossilises ideas and can end by subverting, counteracting and diminishing the very values invoked as most sacred. The West in general, but America in particular, must also face up to this challenge. America demonstrates this character flaw more than any other Western society.

The most hateful of all acts of 'knowledgeable ignorance' is the failure to examine history and to acknowledge that deeds done to others in the name of virtue have actually done great harm. Rewriting history does not wipe the slate clean; indeed, there are ways in which the postmodern passion for rewriting history seeks to disestablish history entirely, rather than address the problems that it bequeathes to today's world. Just as we cannot rely on the strictures and limitations of dead good men to solve today's dilemmas, but have to do our own thinking about the ideas that they had, so too we have to resolve the legacy of problems inherited from their imperfect actions and the operation of their beliefs. We are all sinners, and have all been sinned against. That does not mean that we should abandon investigating and making judgements about which transgressions were most egregious. It is certainly neither excuse nor rationale for doing nothing about the consequences.

Poverty and despair breed frustration. But terrorism is not always the weapon of the weak. It is often the weapon of the alienated, a parody of power, the reverse aspect of the doctrine that might alone is right. This is no justification for terror. But it does demand that we be as ready to condemn the naked use of power to override the rights of others *in all instances*, just as we do in the case of terrorism. It is as unconscionable to justify civilian casualties in the war on terrorism by saying 'War is hell and in war innocents die; too bad', as it is to argue that because bad consequences follow American foreign policy, then any and all Americans are legitimate targets. In a world that lives by double standards, death is also dealt out by double standards. Everyone becomes blind to the one thing that we should all be able to acknowledge: pain and suffering are always the same. There are no acceptable casualties, no forfeitable, dispensable lives. To allow this pernicious doctrine to rule is precisely what makes acts of terror and the practice of state terrorism possible. If terrorism is a parody of power, it cannot be ended by the application of more power tactics.

There are no quick-fix solutions. It is not a matter of merely changing a few policies in a few places. First, these would be palliatives; they might buy time but would not prevent new flashpoints from occurring. Secondly, even to change a few policies in a few places is no easy matter. The most obvious policies, American support for Israel for example, would prove to be the hardest, most intractable problems of all. It is an illusion to think that change will be either swift, easy or painless, and even honestly beginning the process cannot guarantee security and safety. But accepting the *scale* of what is wrong with the way we live together in this world can at least provide the commitment to working for change. Without willingness to think, learn, listen and respect our honest differences, making better policy, or effecting meaningful change, cannot happen.

One of *La Haine*'s main faults is the film's refusal to allow its protagonists some complicity in their own behaviour. They see outsiders in monolithic terms – even those who are trying to help are seen as enemies. People who equate all Americans with the state are guilty of the same crime. It is necessary to appreciate that the United States is a very complex country; and that being American is probably experienced in different ways by different people, depending on their race, ethnicity and ancestry. Moreover, the experience of 'being American' is perhaps rather different than other people's experience of being Chinese or German or Russian. So, simply hating America and the uses and abuses of its power is no answer. It has been, and is, the great excuse. Across the developing world, this great excuse leads moderate, reasonable and concerned people to abandon the political process and disengage from social activism, in the conviction that there is no prospect of achieving significant change. While the silent majority are silent, however valid their reasons, they hand the mantle of action to extremists.

There are many varieties and grades of complicity with the growth of extremism. There is complicity within the Muslim world and other Third World societies, and there is also American complicity. But disengaging from the political process is not a problem of the Third World alone. It also afflicts America.

The lobbying of competing vested interests in the US is not a political debate, it is a whorehouse auction. Foreign policy without effective scrutiny at the ballot-box is a recipe for quasi-elected tyranny. If the abuse of power cannot be restrained in a country that calls itself the shining beacon of liberty and democracy, there is even less hope that wiser counsels will prevail where there is neither democracy nor liberty. This is no excuse, in America or elsewhere, for not taking action to make politics relevant, accountable and responsive. In the world at large as well as within the US, the failure to engage with the problem of America hands victory to the extremists, who answer with the only rhetoric that America seems to understand: violence. We have all participated in the creation of a world in which gun law rules unrestrained.

America too, of course, has its voices of conscience, its smaller structures, its dissenting communities, intellectuals, writers and thinkers concerned about the plight of the rest of the world and seeking to limit American hyperpower and hyper-imperialism. Indeed, we have deliberately quoted and mentioned some of these people throughout the book, as essential testimony that America is not a monolith. There is a moral here for America: the rest of the world is not monolithic either. But our decision to concentrate on American critics of America goes further. Firstly, it suggests that there are new constituencies that can be built across national and cultural boundaries, that there are alternatives to the redundant and inherently dangerous face-off of power tactics. There are more choices than simply being on one side or the other of George W. Bush's 'line in the sand'.

Secondly, and even more importantly, the problems between America and the world exist also within America. America is not the world, nor can America be the world – a one-stop answer to all problems. America itself is fractured, troubled, increasingly split into sundered communities of ideas and interests, suffering an identity crisis on exactly the fault-lines and issues that affect its relations with the rest of the world. We have noted Arthur Schlesinger bemoaning the 'disuniting of America'. Politicians and commentators note the increasingly unbridgeable world-views of the two cultures, liberal and conservative, seeking to pull the nation in opposite directions on issues from abortion to school prayer. We have looked at the rise of Afrocentric education as one among the many permutations of a multicultural vision for re-evaluating identity. And there is the proliferation of survivalist armed militias establishing their own mini-republics in the wilderness, who see the American government as the enemy of freedom, and hate it with a passion; as we have noted, it was the philosophy of the survivalists that motivated the terrorist attack in Oklahoma City. These are the same problems, requiring the same remedies, as those we have pointed to in respect of America's relations with other nations and cultures beyond its shores. America has as much to do to make its own democracy work, to make peace with itself, to mature its own self-identity, as it has to do in coming to terms with the rest of the world.

La Haine begins and ends with the story of a man who falls from a skyscraper. On his way down, he keeps saying, 'So far so good, so far so good'. How people fall, the film seems to be saying, how they come to hate, doesn't really matter. What matters is how you land. The key to a viable and sane future for us all lies in transcending hatred. Since America is both the object and the source of global hatred, it must carry the responsibility of moving us all beyond it. America needs to unwrap itself from the flag, and envelop itself in the prayer of St Francis of Assisi:

> O Master, grant that I may never seek
> So much to be consoled as to console,
> To be understood as to understand,
> To be loved, as to love, with all my soul.[5]

Notes

INTRODUCTION

1. Robert Fisk, 'Fear and Learning in America', *The Independent*, 17 April 2002.
2. Cited in ibid.
3. Beverley Beckham, *Boston Globe*, editorial section, 21 September 2001, p. 35.
4. 'US policies played "significant role" in terror attack', *International Herald Tribune*, 20 December 2001.

CHAPTER ONE

1. Cited by Geraldine Bedell, 'The affairs of state', *The Observer*, Review section, 17 March 2002, p. 10.
2. Richard Brookhiser, *The New York Observer*, 17 September 2001.
3. Thomas Friedman, *Chicago Tribune*, 13 September 2001.
4. Robert Kaplan, NPR, 'Weekend Edition Sunday', 23 September 2001.
5. Karina Rollins, *The American Enterprise*, December 2001.
6. Fareed Zakaria, *Newsweek*, 15 October 2001.
7. Don Feder, *Insight*, 5 November 2001.
8. The television network that broadcasts live from the US House of Representatives and US Senate when they are in session.
9. Also known as the Servicemen's Readjustment Act of 1944, which offered college education to returning veterans of World War II.
10. Victor Davis Hanson, 'Defending the West: Why the Muslims Misjudge Us', *City Journal*, 25 February 2002; *www.opinionjournal.com*
11. Chalmers Johnson, NPR, 'All Things Considered', 12 October 2001.
12. Noam Chomsky, *9-11* (New York: Seven Stories Press, 2001), p. 31.
13. Ibid., p. 23.
14. COINTELPRO is an acronym for the FBI's domestic 'counterintelligence programs', directed largely at left-wing radical groups and aimed at neutralising political dissidents.
15. Dennis Kucinich, 'A prayer for America', 17 February 2002. Speech can be found at: *http://www.house.gov/kucinich/press/speeches.htm*
16. Mary Beard, *London Review of Books*, 4 October 2001, p. 20.
17. Amit Chaudhuri, *London Review of Books*, 4 October 2001, p. 21.
18. Doris Lessing, *Granta*, 77, Spring 2002, p. 54.
19. Harold Pinter, *Granta*, 77, Spring 2002, p. 68.
20. Joe Klein, *The Guardian*, G2, 4 February 2002, p. 2.
21. *The Guardian*, G2, 17 January 2002, p. 1.
22. Anne McLennan, 'War on Terror', *London Free Press* (Canada), 5 November 2001, p. E8.

CHAPTER TWO

1. Peter Brunette, 'Downright Offensive', review for Film.com at *www.film.com*
2. Cited by Thomas Gorguissian in

'Any way they want – A critical review of *Rules of Engagement*', *Al Ahram Weekly*, 479, 27 April 2000.

3. Ibid.

4. Ibid.

5. Ibid.

6. Ibid.

7. 'The Campaign to Subvert Islam as an Ideology and a System', leaflet published by 'Members of Hizb ut-Tahrir in Britain', dated 16 October 2001.

8. Elaine Sciolino, 'A Voice to Calm the Angry Americans', *New York Times*, 17 March 2002.

9. Chris Toensing, *The Boston Globe*, 16 September 2001.

10. Ibid.

11. *Toronto Star* (Ontario edition), 30 November 2001.

12. Edward Said, 'Thought About America', *Al Ahram Weekly*, 28 February–6 March 2002.

13. Ann Coulter, 'This is War', *National Review*, 13 September 2001. Available at *www.nationalreview.com/coulter*

14. Rich Lowry, 'Lots of sentiment for nuking Mecca', *National Review* online, 'Question 1, Follow-up', *www.nationalreview.com/the corner*

15. Said, op. cit.

16. Norman Daniel, *Heroes and Saracens* (Edinburgh: Edinburgh University Press, 1984); and *Islam and the West* (Oxford: One World, 1993; original edition, 1960).

17. Richard Herrnstein and Charles Murray, *The Bell Curve: Intelligence and Class Structure in American Society* (New York: Free Press, 1994).

18. Joseph S. Nye, *The Boston Globe* (third edition), 16 September 2001.

19. Barbara Gunnell, 'Take Cover: Evil is Back', *New Statesman*, 11 February 2002, pp. 16–17.

20. Ronald J. Herring, 'International Education Week: Freedom and Terror', a statement at *www.einaudi.cornell.edu/iew*

21. Josef Joffe, 'Who's Afraid of Mr Big?', *The National Interest*, 64, Summer 2001, p. 43.

22. Bill Clinton, speech at the University of California, San Diego, 14 June 1997.

23. Len Duhl, personal e-mail interview with the authors, 22 February 2002.

CHAPTER THREE

1. The Iran–Contra scandal, revealed in 1986, involved secret US government operations to sell arms to Iran and to the Nicaraguan rebels in contravention of stated US policy and in clear violation of arms export controls, and implicated Reagan administration officials in illegal activities.

2. Johan Galtung, *Searching for Peace* (London: Pluto Press, 2002).

3. Boutros Boutros-Ghali, *Unvanquished: a US–UN Saga* (New York: Random House, 1999).

4. William Blum, *Rogue State* (London: Zed Books, 2001), pp. 185–97.

5. Ibid., p. 198.

6. Cited in Andrew Simms, Tom Big

and Nick Robins, *It's Democracy, Stupid* (London: New Economic Foundation, 2000), p. 6.

7. *Financial Times*, 15 August 2000.
8. *Economist*, 18 September 1999.
9. Ed Mayo, personal interview with the authors, 20 March 2002.
10. Andrew Simms, personal interview with the authors, 20 March 2002.
11. Mayo, op. cit.
12. Jimmy Carter, *Christian Science Monitor*, 29 December 1999.
13. US Agency for International Development (USAID) official website: *www.usaid.gov*
14. Al-Sabban, Larsson, Prodi and Bush quotes from Peter Schwarzer's 'Read my lips' column, 'Kyoto Treaty: Dead – or Comatose?', at *www.theglobalist.com/nor/readlips*
15. Andrew Kimbrell, *The Human Body Shop: The Engineering and Marketing of Life* (Penang: Third World Network, 1993).
16. Jim Dator, personal interview with the authors, 28 February 2002.
17. Ben Bagdikian, *The Media Monopoly* (Boston: Beacon Press, 1983; fifth edition, 1997).
18. Mark Crispin Miller, *The Nation*, 7 January 2002.
19. Phillip Knightley, 'Losing Friends and Influencing People', *Index on Censorship*, January 2002, 31(1), pp. 146–55.
20. Robert W. McChesney, 'Global Media, Neoliberalism and Imperialism', *Monthly Review*, 52, 10 March 2001.
21. Ibid.

CHAPTER FOUR

1. 'Can Charlotte Beers Sell Uncle Sam?', *Time*, 14 November 2001.
2. 'Charlotte Beers' Toughest Sell', *Business Week*, 17 December 2001.
3. *New York Times*, 15 November 2001.
4. Ibid.
5. 'A Travesty of Justice', *New York Times*, 16 November 2001.
6. Geoffrey Robertson QC, 'Justice and Revenge: International Law After Tuesday 11th September 2001', The 25th Thomas Corbishley Memorial Lecture (London: The Wyndham Place Charlemagne Trust, 2001), pp. 7–8.
7. Ibid., p. 9.
8. Ibid., p. 9.
9. William Blum, *Rogue State* (London: Zed Books, 2001), pp. 168–78.
10. Paul Kennedy, 'The Eagle has Landed', *Financial Times*, Weekend section, 3 February 2002.
11. Edward Helmore and Kamal Ahmed, 'Outrage as Pentagon Nuclear Hit List Revealed', *The Observer*, 10 March 2002.
12. Naomi Klein, 'America is not a hamburger', *The Guardian*, 14 March 2002.
13. George Ritzer, 'Obscene from any angle: fast food, credit cards, casinos and consumers', *Third Text*, 51, Summer 2000, pp. 17–28.
14. Margaret Wertheim, personal e-mail interview with the authors, 12 December 2001.

15. Ibid.

16. Philip H Gordon, 'Liberté! Fraternité! Anxiety!', *Financial Times*, Weekend section, 19 January 2002, p. 1.

17. Wertheim, op. cit.

18. 'Youth: The Wilder Ones', *Asiaweek*, 25 May 1994, pp. 24–33.

19. John Sutherland, 'Linguicide: the death of language', *The Independent on Sunday*, LifeEtc section, 10 March 2002, p. 1.

20. Ibid.

21. William Gibson, 'Disneyland With a Death Penalty', *The Observer*, Life section, 14 August 1994.

22. Steve Fuller, personal e-mail interview with the authors, 3 April 2002.

23. Wertheim, op. cit.

24. All quotes from *The Monkey King* publicity material taken from *www.hallmarkent.com*

25. Wertheim, op. cit.

26. Ibid.

27. Ibid.

28. The original Wimpy chain was sold to food group Grand Metropolitan, the owners of Burger King, in 1989, and most were repackaged as Burger Kings. However, some Wimpys are still around. See Paul MacInnes, 'Lunch is for Wimpys', *The Guardian*, 1 February 2002.

CHAPTER FIVE

1. Lewis Lapham, *Waiting for the Barbarians* (London: Verso, 1997), p. 220.

2. Norman Daniel, *Islam and the West: The Making of an Image* (Oxford: One World, 1993), p. 17.

3. Ibid., p. 11.

4. *Islamophobia: A Challenge to Us All*, Report of the Runnymede Trust Commission on British Muslims and Islamophobia, London, 1997.

5. Daniel, *Islam and the West*, p. 17.

6. John Rolfe's letter to Sir Thomas Dale, from the Ashmole MS, reprinted in Philip L. Barbour, *Pocahontas and Her World* (Boston: Houghton Mifflin, 1970), Appendix III, pp. 247–52.

7. John Winthrop, *A Modell of Christian Charity* (1630) (Boston: Collections of the Massachusetts Historical Society, 1838), third series, 7, pp. 31–48.

8. Jimmie Durham, 'Cowboys and ...', *Third Text*, 12, Autumn 1990, pp. 5–20.

9. Ibid.

10. Peter Mathiesson, Foreword to Oren Lyons et al., *Exiled in the Land of the Free* (Santa Fe: Clear Light Publishers, 1992), p. xi.

11. Cited in Lewis Hanke, *Aristotle and the American Indians* (Bloomington: Indiana University Press, 1975), p. 16.

12. Cited in ibid., p. 112.

13. Vince Deloria Jr, 'Indian Law and the Reach of History', *Journal of Contemporary Law*, 4, 1977–8 , pp. 1–13.

14. Cited in Garrett Mattingley, *Renaissance Diplomacy* (Chapel Hill: North Carolina University Press, 1955), p. 290, and in Hanke, op. cit., p. 100.

15. Deloria, op. cit., p. 1.

16. Durham, op. cit., pp. 5–20.

17. Ibid.

18. Daniel K. Inouye, Preface to

Oren Lyons et al., op. cit., p. ix.

19. David E. Wilkins, *American Indian Sovereignty and the US Supreme Court: The Masking of Justice* (Austin: University of Texas Press, 1997), p. 3.

20. Ibid., p. 5.

21. John Rolfe's letter to Sir Edwin Sandys, cited in H. C. Porter, *The Inconstant Savage: England and the North American Indian* (London: Duckworth, 1979), p. 340.

22. The Welsh radical Jacobin, Iolo Morgannwg, who was for a time a shopkeeper, made it a point of honour never to sell sugar produced on slave plantations; he advertised the fact by displaying a large sign reading 'uncontaminated by human gore'.

23. Preface to William Brandon, *The American Heritage Book of Indians* (New York: Dell, 1961).

24. Daniel Lazare, *The Frozen Republic: How the Constitution is Paralyzing Democracy* (New York: Harcourt and Brace, 1996), p. 3.

25. Ibid., p. 9.

26. Cited in Bruce E. Johansen, *Debating Democracy: Native American Legacy of Freedom* (Santa Fe: Clear Light Publishers, 1998), p. 9.

27. Cited in ibid., p. 10.

28. Ibid., p. 187.

29. Arthur M. Schlesinger Jr, *The Disuniting of America: Reflections on a Multicultural Society* (New York: Whittle Books, 1998), p. 134.

CHAPTER SIX

1. Percy Adams, *Travelers and Travel Liars 1660–1800* (New York: Dover, 1980).

2. John L. O'Sullivan, 'Annexation', *United States Magazine and Democratic Review*, July–August 1845, Vol. 17, Issue 085–086, pp. 5–10. Cornell University maintains a searchable archive of this journal at *http://cdl.library.cornell.edu*

3. John L. O'Sullivan, 'The Great Nation of Futurity', *United States Magazine and Democratic Review*, November 1839, Vol. 6, Issue 23, pp. 426–30.

4. Richard Slotkin, *Regeneration Through Violence: The Mythology of the American Frontier 1600–1860* (Middletown, CT: Wesleyan University Press, 1973), p. 25.

5. Cited in Gore Vidal, *The Decline and Fall of the American Empire* (Chicago: Odonian Press, 2000), p. 18.

6. Cited in ibid., p. 16.

7. David Sterritt, *Christian Science Monitor*, 26 September 2001.

8. Richard Slotkin, *The Chronicle of Higher Education*, 28 September 2001.

9. Cited in ibid., p. 29.

10. Lewis Lapham, *Waiting for the Barbarians* (London: Verso, 1997), pp. 29–30.

11. Ibid., p. 31.

12. Ibid., p. 30.

13. Cited in ibid., p. 30.

14. Ibid., p. 32.

15. Slotkin, op. cit. (2001).

CHAPTER SEVEN

1. Bruce Tonn, personal e-mail interview with the authors, 26 February 2002.
2. Chandra Muzaffar, *Human Rights and the New World Order* (Penang: Just World Trust, 1993), p. 13.
3. Walid Amayreh, *The Muslim News*, 29 March 2002, p. 4.
4. Ibid.
5. St Francis of Assisi, 'Make me an Instrument of Your Peace'; see *www.webdesk.com/catholic/prayers*

Select Bibliography

Ahmad, Jalal Ali. *Occidentosis: A Plague from the West* (Berkeley: Mizan Press, 1984).

Ali, Tariq. *The Clash of Fundamentalisms* (London: Verso, 2002).

Appadurai, Arjun. *Modernity at Large: cultural dimensions of globalization* (Minneapolis and London: University of Minnesota Press, 1997).

Bamford, James. *Body of Secrets: Anatomy of the Ultra-Secret National Security Agency* (New York: Doubleday, 2001).

Barber, Benjamin R. *Jihad Vs McWorld* (New York: Times Books, 1995).

Barnet, Richard and John Cavanagh. *Global Dreams: Imperial Corporations and the New World Order* (New York: Simon and Schuster, 1994).

Baudrillard, Jean. *America* (London: Verso, 1988).

Baudrillard, Jean. *Selected Writings*, ed. Mark Poster (Oxford: Polity Press, 1988).

Baudrillard, Jean. *The Transparency of Evil* (London: Verso, 1993).

Baudrillard, Jean. *The Gulf War Did Not Take Place* (Sydney: Power Publications, 1995).

Bauman, Zygmunt. *Modernity and the Holocaust* (Oxford: Polity Press, 1989).

Bauman, Zygmunt. *Postmodern Ethics* (Oxford: Blackwell, 1993).

Bauman, Zygmunt. *Globalization: the human consequences* (Cambridge: Polity Press, 1998).

Blum, William. *Rogue State* (London: Zed Books, 2001).

Bourdieu, Pierre. *Language and Symbolic Power*, ed. John B. Thompson, trans. Gino Raymond and Matthew Adamson (Cambridge: Polity Press, 1991).

Bourdieu, Pierre. *Acts of Resistance: against the new Myths of our time*, trans. Richard Nice (London: Polity Press, 1998).

Bové, José et al. *The World is Not for Sale* (London: Verso, 2001).

Brazier, Chris. *The No-Nonsense Guide to World History* (London: Verso, 2001).

Brzezinski, Zbigniew. *The Grand Chessboard: American Primacy and its Geostrategic Imperatives* (New York: Basic Books, 1997).

Cheikh, Anta Diop. *Civilization or Barbarism: An Authentic Anthropology* (New York: Lawrence Hill Books, 1991).

Chomsky, Noam. *Necessary Illusions* (London: Pluto Press, 1989).

Chomsky, Noam. *Deterring Democracy* (London: Verso, 1991).

Chomsky, Noam. *World Orders, Old and New* (London: Pluto Press, 1994).

Chomsky, Noam. *9-11* (New York: Seven Stories Press, 2001).

Cooley, John K. *Unholy Wars: Afghanistan, America and International Terrorism* (London: Pluto Press, 1999).

Dalby, Andrew. *Language in Danger: How Language Loss Threatens Our Future* (London: Allen Lane, 2002).

Daniel, Norman. *Islam and the West* (Oxford: One World, 1993; original edition, 1960).

Daniel, Norman. *Heroes and Saracens* (Edinburgh: Edinburgh University Press, 1984).

Doherty, Thomas. *Projections of War: Hollywood, American Culture, and World War II* (New York: Columbia University Press, 1993).

Durham, Jimmie. 'Cowboys and …' (*Third Text*, 12, Autumn 1990, pp. 5–20).

Ellwood, Wayne. *The No-Nonsense Guide to Globalisation* (London: Verso, 2001).

Fukuyama, Francis. *The End of History and the Last Man* (London: Hamish Hamilton, 1992).

Granta. *What We Think of America* (London: Granta, 2002).

Halliday, Fred. *Two Hours that Shook the World* (London: Saqi Books, 2002).

Hanke, Lewis. *Aristotle and the American Indians* (Bloomington: Indiana University Press, 1975).

Henry III, William A. *In Defense of Elitism* (New York: Doubleday, 1994).

Hughes, Robert. *Culture of Complaint* (Oxford: Oxford University Press, 1993).

Huntington, Samuel P. 'The clash of civilizations?' (*Foreign Affairs*, 72(3), July/August 1993, pp. 22–49).

Index on Censorship. 'Squeeze on Democracy' (*Index on Censorship*, 31(1), January 2002).

Jennings, Francis. *The Invasion of America* (Chapel Hill: University of North Carolina Press, 1975).

Johansen, Bruce E. *Debating Democracy: Native American Legacy of Freedom* (Santa Fe: Clear Light Publishers, 1998).

Johnson, Chalmers. *Blowback: the costs and consequences of American Empire* (New York: Owl Books, 2000).

Kennedy, Paul. *Preparing for the Twenty-First Century* (London: HarperCollins, 1993).

Kolakowski, Leszek. *Modernity on Endless Trial* (Chicago: University of Chicago Press, 1990).

Kothari, Smitu and Harsh Sethi, eds, *Rethinking Human Rights* (New York: New Horizon Press, 1989).

Lapham, Lewis. *Waiting for the Barbarians* (London: Verso, 1997).

Lawrence, Bruce B. *Shattering the Myth: Islam Beyond Violence* (Princeton: Princeton University Press, 1998).

Lazare, Daniel. *The Frozen Republic: How the Constitution is Paralyzing Democracy* (New York: Harcourt and Brace, 1996).

Lee, Robert. *Orientals* (Philadelphia: Temple University Press, 1999).

London Review of Books. '11 September – Some LRB writers reflect on the reasons and consequences' (*London Review of Books*, 23(19), 4 October 2001, pp. 20–5).

Lyons, Oren et al. *Exiled in the Land of the Free* (Santa Fe: Clear Light Publishers, 1992).

Marchetti, Gina. *Romance and the 'Yellow Peril'* (Berkeley: University of California Press, 1993).

Mazower, Mark. *Dark Continent: Europe's Twentieth Century* (London: Allen Lane, 1998).

Mestrovic, Stjepan. *The Barbarian Temperament* (London: Routledge, 1993).

Moore, Michael. *Stupid White Men* (New York: Regan Books, 2001).

Muzaffar, Chandra. *Human Rights and the New World Order* (Penang: Just World Trust, 1993).

Nandy, Ashis. *Traditions, Tyrannies and Utopias: Essays in Politics of Awareness* (Delhi: Oxford University Press, 1987).

Nandy, Ashis, ed. *Science, Hegemony and Violence* (Delhi: Oxford University Press, 1988).

Nederveen, Jan and Bhiku Parekh, eds. *The Decolonization of Imagination: Culture, Knowledge and Power* (London: Zed Books, 1995).

Norgaard, Richard B. *Development Betrayed* (London: Routledge, 1994).

Pemberton, Jo-Anne. *Global Metaphors* (London: Pluto Press, 2001).

Rieff, David. *Slaughterhouse: Bosnia and the Failure of the West* (London: Vintage, 1995).

Ritzer, George. *The McDonaldization of Society* (Thousand Oaks, CA: Pine Oak Press, 1993).

Said, Edward. *Orientalism* (London: Routledge and Kegan Paul, 1978).

Sardar, Ziauddin and Merryl Wyn Davies. *Distorted Imagination: Lessons from the Rushdie Affair* (London: Grey Seal, 1990).

Sardar, Ziauddin, Merryl Wyn Davies and Ashis Nandy. *Barbaric Others: A Manifesto on Western Racism* (London: Pluto Press, 1993).

Sardar, Ziauddin. *Postmodernism and the Other* (London: Pluto Press, 1998).

Sardar, Ziauddin, ed. *Rescuing All Our Futures* (Westport, CT: Praeger Publishers, 1998).

Sardar, Ziauddin. *Orientalism* (Buckingham: Open University Press, 1999).

Sardar, Ziauddin. *The A to Z of Postmodern Life* (London: Vision, 2002).

Schlesinger Jr, Arthur M. *The Disuniting of America: Reflections on a Multicultural Society* (New York: Whittle Books, 1998).

Schlosser, Eric. *Fast Food Nation* (London: Allen Lane, 2002).

Seabrook, Jeremy. *Victims of Development: Resistance and Alternatives* (London: Verso, 1993).

Shaheen, Jack. *The TV Arab* (Bowling Green, OH: Bowling Green State University Popular Cultural Press, 1985).

Shaheen, Jack. 'The Hollywood Arab' (*Journal of Popular Film and Television*, 14(4), 1987, pp. 148–57).

Shintaro, Ishihara. *The Japan That Can Say No* (New York: Simon and Schuster, 1991).

Shohat, Ella and Robert Stam. *Unthinking Eurocentrism* (London: Routledge, 1994).

Slotkin, Richard. *Regeneration Through Violence: The Mythology of the American Frontier 1600–1860* (Middletown, CT: Wesleyan University Press, 1973).

Slotkin, Richard. *The Fatal Environment: The Myth of Frontier in the Age of Industrialization 1800–1890* (Norman, OK: University of Oklahoma Press, 1998).

Slotkin, Richard. *Gunfighter Nation: The Myth of Frontier in Twentieth-Century America* (Norman, OK: University of Oklahoma Press, 1998).

Stinnett, Robert B. *Day of Deceit: The Truth About FDR and Pearl Harbor* (New York: Touchstone Books, 2001).

Stivers, Richard. *The Culture of Cynicism* (Oxford: Blackwell, 1994).

Swift, Richard. *The No-Nonsense Guide to Democracy* (London: Verso, 2002).

Tester, Keith. *The Inhuman Condition* (London: Routledge, 1995).

Tomlinson, John. *Cultural Imperialism* (London: Pinter, 1991).

Vidal, Gore. *The Decline and Fall of the American Empire* (Chicago: Odonian Press, 2000).

Wilkins, David E. *American Indian Sovereignty and the US Supreme Court: The Masking of Justice* (Austin: University of Texas Press, 1997).

Wollen, Peter. 'Cinema/Americanism/The Robot', in James Naremore and Patrick Brantlinger, eds. *Modernity and Mass Culture* (Bloomington: Indiana University Press, 1991).

World Bank. *Adjustment in Africa* (Oxford: Oxford University Press, 1994).

Žižek, Slavoj. *The Sublime Object of Desire* (London: Verso, 1989).

Acknowledgements

We would like to thank Lotfi Hermi, Shamim Miah, Jan Mair, Sohail Inayatullah, Sean Cubitt, Sujit Patwardhan, Scott Crawford, David Peat, Kirk Junker, Michael Clark and other friends for their valuable advice and comments. Thanks also to Duncan Heath for his careful and patient editing, and Jeremy Cox for his constant nagging. Merryl Wyn Davies would like to thank her mother for cheerfully enduring parental neglect during the writing of this book. Ziauddin Sardar would like to offer the same olive branch to his kids.

Index